MW00398638

HERE'S WHAT PEOPLE ARE SAYING ABOUT *LIMITLESS: DEFY THE ORDINARY* BY ERIC PETREE

In a moment in history that seems to be defined by barriers and restrictions, the message in *Limitless: Defy the Ordinary* is like a renewal of the mind—an awakening of the spirit to the nature of Christ that resides within us. Pastor Petree's engaging words are inviting, accessible, and just what we need right now.

—Tommy Barnett, Global Pastor, Dream City Church,
Phoenix, Arizona, Co-Pastor, Los Angeles Dream Center

Nobody wants to be average. No one wants to be an average mother, father, worker—an average *anything*. We were born for the extraordinary but often settle for ordinary. In his latest book, *Limitless: Defy the Ordinary,* my friend Eric Petree challenges us to break all limits and live the extraordinary lives we were born to live.

—Sam Chand, Leadership Consultant
and Author of *Leadership Pain*

WOW … my friend Eric Petree has done it! I hope you will invest in yourself and allow the wisdom of *Limitless: Defy the Ordinary* to enter your world. It's time to learn how to navigate the journey from "here to there."

—Pastor Charles Nieman, Abundant Living
Faith Center, El Paso, Texas

Truly impactful books are not just written; they are first lived—then written. If I know anyone with such *Limitless* experiences, it would be Eric Petree.

Pastor Eric has rolled up his sleeves and gotten his hands dirty in the trenches. He is a tried and true warrior leader who has pushed through the lines of resistance to taste the sweet victories of accomplishment. If anyone is qualified to speak on *Limitless, Defying the Ordinary*, it is he. Take the step to start making better life choices and push yourself to limitless possibilities by reading this book.

—Bryan Cutshall, Th.D., President, International School of the Word, President, Church Trainer, Chattanooga, Tennessee

Pastor Eric guides you easily into the limitless power of God! I am so thankful for Pastor Eric and his example of leading people to God's forgiveness and limitless power!

—Matthew Barnett, *New York Times* Best-Selling Author, Co-Founder of The Dream Center, Los Angeles, California

Pastor Eric's writing will change your "bottom-up" perspective into a "top-down" view for your future, aligning your vision with God's plan for your life!

—Dr. Louis Kayatin, Marriage and Family Consultant, Keynote Speaker, Estero, Florida

If you want different results, do not do the same things," isn't just a pop-culture catchphrase; it's a quote by Albert Einstein that my friend Eric captures the very essence of in his book, *Limitless: Defy the Ordinary.* Faith, in and of itself, breaks the box of mundane living and presents us with the promise of life more abundant. If you want to be inspired, motivated, and moved to dream again, this book will help you do just that!

—Ronnie Harrison, Pastor, The Kingdom Center, Louisville, Kentucky

Limitless

Defy the
Ordinary

Scripture quotations marked KJV are taken from the King James Version of the Bible. Public domain. | Scripture quotations marked NIV are taken from the Holy Bible, New International Version®, NIV®. Copyright © 1973, 1978, 1984, 2011 by Biblica, Inc.™ Used by permission of Zondervan. All rights reserved worldwide. www.zondervan.com. The "NIV" and "New International Version" are trademarks registered in the United States Patent and Trademark Office by Biblica, Inc.™ | Scripture quotations marked NKJV are taken from the New King James Version®. Copyright © 1982 by Thomas Nelson. Used by permission. All rights reserved. | Scripture quotations marked ESV are taken from the Holy Bible, English Standard Version, Copyright © 2001 by Crossway, a publishing ministry of Good News Publishers. Used by permission. All rights reserved.

For foreign and subsidiary rights, contact the author.

Cover design by: Joe DeLeon
Cover photo by: Adrian Payne Photography

ISBN: 978-1-954089-09-9   1 2 3 4 5 6 7 8 9 10

Printed in the United States of America

Defy the
Ordinary

ERIC PETREE

AVAIL

ACKNOWLEDGMENTS

For the love of my life, Kimberly, you would not give up until I believed in myself as much as you do. You have walked with me through every challenge and stood by my side in every victory. You have refused to allow me to live a mediocre life, always inspiring me to reach for more. We've always broken the limits together, and this one represents the first of a million more. I love you more than cheese coneys and chocolate.

For my daughter, Saige, I am and always will be your biggest fan. Thank you for being mine. It's you and me, kid!

For my son, Rush, you are truly limitless. You might only be two at the time of this writing, but you've already given us a lifetime of joy. Dream big dreams, son. Nothing is impossible!

For my parents, Leon and Karen, may this represent the sunrise of your sacrifices, your faithfulness fulfilled, and the power of your prayers.

FOREWORD

Time is a relentless adversary, and as it forges ahead, I am haunted by questions, such as this one: "What will become of gospel preaching among those who are filling pulpits in the years to come?" As a stellar representative of the new generation of preachers, Pastor Eric Petree of Citygate Church in the greater Cincinnati area gives me tremendous confidence as I look to the future. In him, I see the hallmarks of someone whom God has truly touched with His anointing. He is imaginative, creative, and effective in handling God's Word's timeless truths and crafting life-transforming messages for everyone looking for reality and relevance in a postmodern world.

Uniquely gifted as a leader who thinks beyond the boundaries of religious rudiments and the current culture, Pastor Petree is wise beyond his years in his approach to bringing the gospel of Jesus Christ to those who so desperately need it.

My pastor and mentor, Dr. Lester Sumrall, told me, "Writing is the key to longevity." In this age of electronically mediated communication that is here and gone in a moment, that advice is more pertinent than ever. I have done my best to impress that truth upon the new generation of preachers everywhere I go.

As a true son in the faith and a proud graduate of Valor Christian College, Eric Petree continues that legacy. In his book,

Limitless: Defy the Ordinary, he shares unique insights in his capable and inimitable style that will challenge and change you.

Eric is not only a loving husband to Kim and a wonderful father to Saige and Rush but also a humble pastor who possesses the heart of a servant and desires to bring effective and lasting change to the kingdom of God. Watching his growth from a young man in Bible college with a passion for God to a successful pastor and soul winner has been a blessing in my personal life. I can attest that Eric's preaching ministry has blessed thousands, including me. Therefore, I could not be more pleased to recommend his writing to you as well.

—Dr. Rod Parsley
Pastor and Founder,
World Harvest Church
Columbus, Ohio

CONTENTS

INTRODUCTION

Now to him who is able to do far more abundantly than all that
we ask or think, according to the power at work within us.
—Ephesians 3:20 (ESV)

When God painted the first brushstroke of creation upon the heavens, He set a precedent that is, has always been, and will ever be—He is a God without limitation. His creativity molded the earth, hung the stars, and shaped the cosmos. His imagination painted the zebra, creatures of the ocean depths, and the birds that soar in the skies. His love birthed man and woman from dust, placed a longing for Him within their hearts, and gifted them with abundance.

From before the first sunrise to this very moment, our God has demonstrated that He is without boundaries. He is the God of the impossible. He is limitless.

While many of us probably believe that theoretically, we tend to live lives bound by our earthly estimation of what is or is not possible. From the time we are born, we are given boundaries, limitations and told to dream only as far as we can see.

We live lives of restriction rather than abundance. We wrestle with our weaknesses instead of exploring our strengths and testing the extent to which we can impact the world around us.

But that is not the life God intended you to live. He created you in His image. Therefore, if He is truly limitless, so too are you.

So why do you feel constrained? Why is it that you feel inadequate?

When you live a life within the boundaries of man, you learn to survive. When things are good, your head stays above water. When things go south, because you have been living without margin, you follow suit. Before you know it, you aren't even living a life of restriction; you are living within a deficit.

I've been there. I have wrestled with loss, hurt, rejection, anxiety, and fear. There have been moments that I have doubted the feet God has given me to traverse this thing called life, much less the road on which I'm traveling. However, over the years, I have prayerfully and intentionally attempted to live a life that reflects Ephesians 3:20. I have tried, not without failure along the way, to trust that my circumstances do not impact my limitless Father's ability to do the impossible in my life.

My hope is that you can do the same. Rather than being consumed by the struggles you see before you, reframe your lens, strive for a new perspective that removes those obstacles that have been holding you back, while revealing the infinite possibilities of a life lived hand-in-hand with our Heavenly Father.

Never doubt that our limitless God is at work doing what He does best—redeeming impossible situations while refining those who dare to live for more.

I hope you will find inspiration to live a deeper life within these pages, more fully invested in your unique God-given purpose. I hope you will find a kindred spirit who knows grief and loss and has experienced healing and wishes for you to do the same.

As long as we walk on this fallen earth, we will encounter impossible situations and treacherous boundaries. Yet, for those who know and love God, let us walk with our head high, heart pointed toward heaven, each foot a step closer to the limitless life our limitless God has created for you and me, right here and right now.

You were not designed to survive. You were created to thrive.

chapter 1

GO FLY A KITE

Breaking the Limit of Small Thinking

Every good and perfect gift is from above.
—James 1:17a (ESV)

The optimist pleasantly ponders how high his kite will fly, while the pessimist woefully wonders how soon his kite will fall.
—William Ward[1]

The breeze was warm and picking up just enough for the inaugural flight of the brand-new kite my parents had given me. This was no ordinary kite. It wasn't a diamond or a triangle or any other arbitrary shape. It was a full-on bald eagle. A sturdy wood frame supported it, and I knew that I would conquer the skies above within minutes.

---

1   William Ward. Retrieved on December 27, 2020, from quotefancy.com. Website: https:// quotefancy.com/quote/933928/William-Arthur-Ward-The-optimist-pleasantly-ponders-how- high-his-kite-will-fly-theSpeaker.

As I readied the reel, my mom was with me, letting out the string as my magnificent eagle climbed higher and higher. For just a brief moment, I knew that God must have bestowed special kite-flying abilities upon my young soul because this kite seemed like it was on a one-way trip to the heavens above. Then it made a U-turn.

The pressure that was keeping the kite high above my head suddenly became too much. The stress of the extreme height snapped that indestructible eagle frame like a matchstick, and even more quickly than it had climbed up into the sky, it plummeted back towards Earth.

I was devastated. Then, my mom stepped in and worked her mom magic with super glue and duct tape. And wouldn't you know … that kite flew again.

Do you remember when you were a kid, and your kite could fly to the moon and back? Or you could one day be President of the United States? Or an Olympian? Do you remember when you believed with your whole heart that the sky was the limit, and anything was possible?

Our younger selves knew how to dream! Not yet jaded by mistakes, missteps, or lost opportunities, we visualized ourselves on top of the world. While we didn't necessarily know how we were going to get there, it was never a question of "if." It was always a matter of "when."

Somewhere along the way, though, we start to lose sight of those dreams. We begin letting circumstances and cultural norms dictate our pursuits. Your dream of becoming president is soon replaced with a practical plan to become a regional manager. Instead of aiming for the Olympics, you settle with going to the gym a few times a week. Over time, one day rolls into the next, as does the one after that, and before you can even process it, you're pushing 40 or 50 with a handful of unfulfilled dreams and no clear direction,

In the book of Proverbs, Solomon writes that without vision, people will perish. In this context, the word "vision" is actually "dream." When he says people will perish, the literal translation is that people will wander aimlessly through scattered lives.

The enemy will do everything he can to put a cap on your limitless dream. He'll go so far as to make you forget you ever had a dream at all, leaving you listless and making you question whether you have or have ever had anything to offer to others. That is the beginning of a slippery slope. Once you convince yourself that no one else needs you or wants what you have to offer, you're likely to isolate, disconnect from those people and things in which you used to find value. You put your dreams on a shelf, push them to the back, and leave them there, convinced they are out of reach. The only thing worse than never reaching your dreams, however, is never having one at all.

No matter how persuasive you are in convincing yourself that your dreams are impossible or nonexistent, the truth is that God has given you a dream—a limitless one that can't be contained within walls or below a ceiling. He has equipped you with the desire and the tools necessary to fulfill His dream for your life. It's time to take the limits off your dream.

Do you know what your dream is? Do you believe that God can help you achieve it, or are you just waiting to watch it crash and fall? Before you dismiss your dream, keep this in mind: Every dream matters. No matter how big or small, every dream matters to God. Every dream mothers and fathers have for their children matters. Every dream husbands and wives have for their marriage matters. Every dream a business owner has for his or her business matters. Even your broken dreams matter.

Here's the thing—you have to decide to legitimize your dreams. You have to choose anticipation over resignation. You have to keep your eyes lifted to the sky, not down to the ground or behind you.

The writer and scholar William Ward wrote, "The optimist pleasantly ponders how high his kite will fly while the pessimist woefully wonders how soon his kite will fall."

If you're ready to be an optimist, to ponder how high your dreams can fly, consider the basics of kite flying a template for your dream chasing.

KITE FLYING 101
Fly Against the Wind

Kites, like airplanes, need resistance to go higher. God-sized dreams will always face resistance. The enemy isn't going to passively allow your dream to take off. He will do everything he can to ground you and your dream. The harder he tries to keep you out of the skies, though, the higher God can carry you.

In 1 Corinthians 16:9 (ESV), the apostle Paul wrote, "For a wide door for effective work has opened to me, and there are many adversaries."

God opened the door for Paul; in the same way, He will open up dreams for you. When that door was opened, the adversaries arrived. Note the order. The door didn't open because of the adversaries; the adversaries came because of the door.

If you are suddenly facing a host of problems and challenges in your life, chances are your dream existed before these issues arose. The trials showed up to stop your vision, but God can use them to elevate the dream. Resistance is required to go higher. Have you been facing resistance? It's easy to assume that when resistance arises, it must be a sign that God is not in the dream. If He were, surely it would be easier, right?

Think for a moment about the time Jesus told the disciples to get in the boat. When they were in the middle of the sea, a storm hit, and Jesus walked on water. Sometimes, resistance is present to show you where God wants you to be.

Find A Friend

I have great memories of flying a kite as a kid. I'd go out in the backyard, prop the kite up, and then do that slow walk back. It has to be just right, so you can pull it and take off. Without fail, no matter how careful I was, it would always fall to the ground. Then I'd go inside and get my mom or dad and ask for help. I needed someone else to help me get the kite in the air.

Sometimes, God brings along dreamers with whom you can connect to give your dream a head start. It's always easier to move forward with two people. In Matthew 18:19 (ESV), Jesus said, "Again, I say to you, if two of you agree on earth about anything they ask, it will be done for them by my father in heaven."

Maybe the only thing keeping your dream on the ground is the absence of a partner or friend you can agree with and work with to move your dream forward.

If you've ever seen two kids in a field with only one kite, the kid without a kite can say all day long that he doesn't want or need one. But once the other kid gets that kite up in the air, kid number one is going to start asking to hold the string for a little bit or just to try it for a while. He'll then go home and ask Mom and Dad for a kite.

If you don't feel like you have a dream, maybe you need to check the people you're hanging around. Challenge yourself to hang around people who have some kites in the air, who have dreams of their own. If you are around other people's dreams, you're more inclined to go to the Father and ask for a dream of your own.

Be Aware of Your Environment

You probably already know that a successful kite launch and flight require a lot of space. It would be next to impossible to get one up in the air if you don't have a large area in which you can run and help generate the resistance necessary for takeoff. The caveat—there will likely be stones to trip on, low-hanging branches to run into, and pot-holes tailor-made for twisting your ankles.

Given the obstacles that lie before you on your kite's playing field, and your personal history of tripping, falling, or stumbling, it might seem logical to keep your eyes on the ground to avoid bodily harm. When you do that, though, you are taking your eyes off the kite. You don't know if it's going up, down, left, right, with the wind or against it. By the time you reestablish a line of sight with your kite, you likely won't have enough time to recover before it spirals to the ground.

The same idea applies to your dreams. If some problem or circumstance enters your life and pulls your eyes away from God, chances are you'll develop a habit of looking down for the next crisis or tragedy. Just like the kite, when you take your eyes off of God and the dream He has given you, it won't be long before it too is tangled and plummeting to the ground.

And when you take your eyes off your kite, it isn't long until your kite gets tangled, and it's unable to fly.

So how do you keep the kite—your dream—aloft while maneuvering the landscape beneath your feet? You start by first acknowledging the imperfections of the field. Problems are going to come. Mistakes are going to happen. Failures are inevitable. Don't let these setbacks divert your attention from the dream God has given you. You can't live a full life if you're always looking down. James 1:17a (NIV) says, "Every good and perfect gift comes from above."

When my daughter, Saige, was little and flying a kite for the first time, her eyes were glued to that kite. The possibility of a pothole or other hindrance hadn't even crossed her mind. Why? Because Daddy was right there beside her, keeping an eye out for obstacles, ready to catch her if she fell.

If my daughter could put such unequivocal trust in me, how much more should the rest of us trust our Heavenly Father to guide us along the way and catch us when we stumble? Psalms 37:23-24 (ESV) says, "The steps of a man are established by the Lord when he delights in his way; though he falls, he shall not be cast headlong, for the Lord upholds his hand."

Choose to believe that God will help you navigate the obstacles before you. Align your dreams with heaven, raise your eyes, and trust that, even if you stumble, He will pick you up and set your feet back on solid ground.

Adapt to Deal With Changing Conditions

As long as you occupy this earth, you can rely upon the inevitability of change. Your family structure or home may change. You may switch professions. You may encounter a global pandemic that forces most of the globe to adapt to radical life changes. While your circumstances change, though, your dreams never will; at least, they never have to. If you can commit yourself to flexibility, adaptability, and grace, you will not just survive the ups and downs of life always in flux; you will thrive because of them.

Have you ever watched an expert kite flier at work? I'm not just talking about people in the park. I'm talking about the professional kite fliers, the kind who win competitions, join the American Kite-fliers Association, and attend conventions with fellow kite enthusiasts. These people know what they're doing.

I once saw such a guy on the beach. His kite was performing stunts that rivaled a Blue Angels stunt show. His kite was doing loops, taking dives, and all the other things I'd always wished I could do with a kite. What caught my attention more than the tricks, however, was the way this guy was moving. He wasn't standing still. He was constantly moving with the kite, adjusting for variations in the wind and the kite's direction the whole time, never taking his eyes off the kite.

If you want to keep your dream alive, you have to get moving. Once you start moving, you can't stop. I read a statistic the other day that, on average, retirees only live three to five years after they've left the workforce. What happened? They lost their dream. They used to have a reason to wake up in the morning. They used to have a purpose, and chances are, that purpose used to be correlated with a dream they had once upon a time.

With no job to go to, no obligations to fulfill, it doesn't take long for one to sink into a mundane routine of inconsequential, uninspiring actions. We weren't made to live this way. Our bodies, hearts, and minds were meant to be filled with intention and meaning. Without those, without dreams to chase, the will to live all but disappears.

While this is most prevalent in seniors, anyone at any age can lose a dream, give up on purpose, and abandon intention.

Lucky for us, God is able and willing to refresh those dreams at any age. He can revive the drive we used to have; He can make your future even more fulfilling than the past you left behind. Your latter will be greater than your former. You're going to do more in the last half of your life than you did in the first half of your life. Don't allow changing circumstances to nullify your dream. Seek God's will, adapt, and don't stop until you get your vision back.

TROUBLESHOOTING

Remember my kite flying adventure with the eagle kite that couldn't withstand the pressure? Chances are, you too have had a kite flying adventure go awry. So, what do you do after a fall? You troubleshoot. You identify the reason for the mishap, and you correct it.

One of the most fundamental reasons a kite will stay grounded or have minimal airtime is the absence of a strong wind. In that case, when the skies are still, you have to do some extra work to get that kite in the air. You have to run. You have to create your own wind until the real thing shows up.

Confession time: I don't always feel like preaching week after week. Sometimes, I don't feel even the slightest breeze or the smallest amount of momentum to compel me to the pulpit. When that happens, I have to act like I'm trying to fly without a breeze. I have to muster up some faith and start running, and I have to keep running until the passion returns.

Habakkuk 2:2 (ESV) reads, "Write the vision; make it plain on tablets, so he may run who reads it." Even when I don't feel the wind, I know it's coming, and I will keep running until it gets here.

Get the Weight Off

When there isn't a strong wind to carry your kite into the air, sometimes running may not generate quite enough momentum to get it going. In that case, you might need to remove any excess weight that's holding the kite back. Maybe this means removing a tail or some other embellishment. If an element is causing more harm than good, if it weighs you down when you need to be lifted up, it needs to go.

I love what Paul wrote, as recorded in Hebrews 12:1 (ESV): "Therefore, since we are surrounded by so great a cloud of witnesses, let us also lay aside every weight, and sin which clings so closely, and let us run with endurance the race that is set before us."

You can't run well or very far when you've got excess baggage. If you are hoping to infuse life into your dream but haven't let go of the sin attached to it, you'll likely be disappointed. God doesn't blow His breath on a dream while you are mired in choices, relationships, and actions that aren't supposed to be a part of your life. If you are ready to soar, you have to drop the weight.

Don't Let Go

One of my earliest kite flying memories didn't have a terribly happy ending. I was just a little kid, standing in the back yard, my kite in the air, and then something distracted me just long enough for the reel to be yanked out of my hand. If you've ever had the pleasure of trying to chase down a runaway kite, you know very well that it's no small feat. You might as well be trying to catch a mad squirrel that knows your backyard much better than you do.

Now, your kite is flopping in the breeze all on its own, the strings are getting tangled, and you have no way to keep that kite away from power lines and trees. One of the greatest pop-culture heroes of all time knows this type of incident all too well. Poor Charlie Brown. He had a relentless enemy in the kite-eating tree. Every time he tried to take to the skies, the tree was ready and waiting, eager to end Charlie Brown's fun once again.

Limitless | *Defy the Ordinary*

There is yet at least one more way you can inadvertently get rid of a kite. One day, I was having a really good kite day. It was going higher than I'd ever flown one before. They had to divert air traffic due to my mad kite flying skills. Suddenly, in the midst of my feeling proud of myself, I noticed that the kite started yanking harder. The higher it went, the stronger the winds became—until the string broke utterly, leaving me with an empty reel and my kite free to wander the skies above. I never saw that kite again.

Just as quickly as a kite can escape us, so too can our dreams. Sometimes, we're frantically chasing something—anything—for the singular reason of wanting to hold on to something. This can lead us to bad relationships, professional blunders, and a lot of unrequited dreams. When we run after things that were never supposed to be in our lives in the first place, we don't have time, space, or the energy to acquire the things that should.

Other times, just like the kite that flew too high, we encounter strong winds. The higher we get and the more we acquire, the enemy is equally inclined to clip our strings and send our dreams tossing and turning in the wind, never to be seen again.

Suppose that's your story. If your dream has gotten away from you, good news! God wants to reconnect you to your dream. Billy Graham used to tell the story of a little boy flying his kite on a beautiful, windy day. The little boy's kite went up and up until the clouds entirely hid it. A man walked by and asked the little boy what he was doing. The little boy replied, "I'm flying a kite."

The man looked up in the sky and back to the boy and said, "Are you? How do you know? I can't see anything up there."

The little boy looked back at the man and said, "Yeah, you can't see it, but every now and then I feel a tug on the string."

You may be convinced that your dream has gotten away from you. But there's something that wakes you up in the middle of the night, interrupts your day, rarely leaves your mind. That's the tug of the dream you thought was long gone. God is reconnecting you to the dream, saying, "Even though it left your eyes, it was never out of my sight."

The Big Idea

It's never too late to reconnect with your dream.
What dream are you mourning the loss of? Do you think
God can revive its spark within you? If you know your
dream, what is holding you back from letting it soar?

Prayer

Lord, thank You for being a limitless God who bestows limitless dreams on the hearts and minds of His children. Help me rediscover the dreams I have let fly away. Give me discernment, wisdom, and energy to reengage with the dream You gave to me. Help my eyes remain focused on You regardless of circumstance, fear, or uncertainty. Thank You for never taking Your eyes off of me or my dreams.

chapter 2

HERE TO THERE

Breaking the Limit of Comfort

Where there is no vision, the people will perish.
—Proverbs 29:18a (KJV)

We choose to go to the Moon in this decade and do the other things, not because they are easy, but because they are hard.
—John F. Kennedy[2]

Brandon grew up with all eyes on him. At least, as one preacher's kid and another preacher's grandkid, that's how it felt. There were always certain expectations and a degree of accountability that felt somewhat stifling. Once he got to college, Brandon decided it was time to have some fun. He went to parties, started drinking, and one night made a decision that would completely alter the course of his life—he smoked his first joint. Soon, weed was a normal part of life. It wasn't long before he started experimenting with harder drugs. Over the next 12 years, his addictions robbed him of health, stability, relationships,

---

2   Kennedy, J. F. Retrieved on December 13, 2020, from John F. Kennedy Podium. Website: https://spacecenter.org/exhibits-and-experiences/starship-gallery/kennedy-podium/.

and dignity. When he landed in jail for having drugs in his car, he knew something had to change. He couldn't continue living a life like this.

He needed to get out. He needed to reach someplace else. While he wasn't sure what that would look like, he knew if he stayed where he was, he would die. It was time to leave "here" and go "there." He didn't know how, but he knew the kind of life that he wanted. He could picture the person he hoped to become. And that vision, that longing to go "there," was the first critical step on his journey to turn things around.

The Bible says that, "Where there is no vision, the people will perish" (Proverbs 29:18a, KJV).

We tend to be visual creatures. Images, even those inside the mind, can compel us to do or think one way or another. Maybe that's why we are told that we absolutely must have a vision for our lives from the time we are old enough to play in a sandbox. What we want to be, who we want to be, hinges on the presence or absence of vision.

While I don't disagree, I find it a little strange that with all the emphasis on having a vision, no one ever says much about finding your vision. Imagine you have coffee with someone who asks, "If you had unlimited funds, unlimited resources, and all the time in the world, what would you do?"

Now imagine you utter something vague or shrug an "I don't know" their way. That conversation is now over. Too bad. Turns out, they had a blank check with your name on it. But you had nothing for them to fund, so they pocketed it for another idea another day. You can't support a dream that doesn't exist. Business investors don't invest in shoulder shrugs and indecision. I've often thought that when it seems like God is withholding things from us, it's not due to a lack of faith but rather to a lack of vision. Why would God provide for something for which you have no vision?

John Maxwell said, "Where there is no hope in the future, there is no power in the present."[3]

It took Brandon a long time to reach a point at which he even wanted a future without his addiction. His days were listless, without direction and purpose, enslaved to something that was clouding his line of sight, blurring the images of tomorrow to the point where tomorrow didn't even matter.

When he finally hit the lowest point, he realized he didn't want to stay put any longer. He had a glimpse of a different life and, just like that, his present regained some power. He had something to aim for. He could begin to care enough about his life to invest in what it would take to start the journey from "here" to "there."

In 1962, President John F. Kennedy delivered one of his most powerful and memorable speeches. It was the height of the Cold War between the United States and the Soviet Union. Each side knew that whoever could master space first—send satellites, shuttles, and people out of the atmosphere—would be the victor. And America was losing.

Then, Kennedy said these words: "We choose to go to the Moon in this decade and do the other things, not because they are easy, but because they are hard."[4]

---

3 Maxwell, J. Retrieved on December 17, 2020, from quotefancy.com. Website: https://quotefancy.com/quote/841274/John-C-Maxwell-Where-there-is-no-hope-in-the-future-there-is-no-power-in-the-present.

4 Kennedy, J. F. (2017). President John F. Kennedy: "We choose to go to the moon." The Washington Post. Retrieved on December 17, 2020. Website: https://www.washingtonpost.com/video/national/president-john-f-kennedys-we-choose-to-go-to-the-moon-speech/2017/10/09/881ac76e-ad1d-11e7-9b93-b97043e57a22_video.html.

In July 1969, Neil Armstrong replied with, "That's one small step for man; one giant leap for mankind,"[5] from the surface of the moon.

We had done it. We had gone from "here" to "there"—from Earth to the moon. How did we do it? Well, it wasn't a straight shot. Like any significant undertaking, those who raced to the Moon did it in stages, one step at a time. The process revealed three things that are relevant to anyone trying to get from here to there.

Little things can defeat big futures. Just like our daily habits influence our overall health and quality of life, the smallest, mundane decisions we make will drastically impact the outcome. While the Apollo 1 astronauts were training, several tiny factors—pure oxygen environment, the use of Velcro, which is incredibly flammable, the hatch door's position—led to a catastrophic fire that killed Roger Chaffee, Gus Grissom, and Ed White.

The tragedy exposed the danger of overlooking the little things. If you want to move closer to your "there," you have to pay attention to the little things—your self-talk, the way you spend free time, the way you invest your resources, even the way you take care of your health. Any one of these can pull your future out from under you before you even realize you're falling.

What you see "there" will determine whether or not you leave "here." You have to know where you're going, or you'll never go anywhere. If you're not looking for and visualizing the destination, there is zero incentive to try to reach it. Brandon could see that those who lived without an active addiction were happier, healthier, and more hopeful. What he saw while looking at them was in such sharp

---

5   Armstrong, N. (1969). Retrieved on December 17, 2020. Website: https://www.nasa.gov/mission_pages/apollo/apollo11.html.

contrast with what he saw in the mirror that it gave him the push he needed to start the journey.

Kennedy's call to action painted a vision of human achievement, success, and victory. He made the destination real and exciting and compelling. He gave the country a reason to go from "here" to "there."

How you get there will determine how long you stay there. In other words, there are no shortcuts to the Moon, or to sobriety, or debt elimination, or weight loss, or any other goal you can think of. You might be able to cut some corners here and there, gloss over some regulations, sneak through a couple of loopholes. But if you choose to do that, instead of putting in the work, earning the goal, chances are, if you make it to the destination, your tenure will be short because you won't know how to live in your vision.

You have to take each step for yourself. Earn your goals. Otherwise, "there" will send you straight back to where you started—not because you're unworthy of staying; you're just unprepared and ill-equipped.

Most of us would agree that it's almost impossible to imagine living in a world where no man had walked on the Moon. Honestly, though, it wasn't that long ago. Can you imagine what people must have been thinking back then? Hearing that we would do whatever it took to conquer the heavens must have sounded ridiculous, but also crazy exciting.

Imagine the opening day of your very first business, or the publication date of your first book, or even your first day of school. It would be so exciting! You'd be full of energy and adrenaline and ready to take on the world.

That's what I call beginning momentum. Everything is fun at first. Even working out or starting a new diet feels great on day one. Your vision of the life, health, or job you want is still crystal clear, and you're finally making it happen.

But there's a reason most gyms make their annual budgets in January. Come week two or month two—sometimes even day two—what had seemed so remarkable now seems tedious and requires just a bit too much effort. The time you'd allocated to your new endeavor is somehow being increasingly consumed by Netflix or other people or other problems that you are choosing to focus on, rather than focus on that dream that was lighting up your world just a little while ago.

This, my friend, is called the Nothing Zone, and it is where dreams go to die. The start-up momentum has faded, you can still see your old life in your rear-view mirror, and the distance between you and your vision seems to be growing or stagnant. Either way, it sure doesn't seem to be shrinking.

The Apollo 13 Mission is probably one of the most well-known space disasters (thank you, Ron Howard and Tom Hanks). A few days into the flight, there was an explosion on the ship that crippled the spacecraft, eliminated the possibility of a moon landing, and put the three astronauts' lives on the line.

Similarly, when Moses led the people out of Egypt, they were over-the-top ecstatic that they were finally free and heading to the Promised Land—but then the Egyptians came after them. God parted the Red Sea; they walked through, excitement restored, and were free once again—until they reached the desert. For 40 years, they wandered through the wilderness. Over time, Moses' promises of milk, honey, freedom, and happiness seemed like a pipe dream.

Just like those astronauts, they had entered the Nothing Zone. For the men in space, their destination, their promised land, was now out of reach. For the people of Israel, the Promised Land seemed so far out of reach that they reached the point most of us do when the momentum runs out.

That's when we start asking questions.

Was this worth it?

Did we need to leave "here"?

We've never been "there." How do we know we'll even like it?

Should we go back?

Can you imagine, even after 400 years of slavery, how many Hebrews had had it with this journey into freedom? They were willing to go back into oppression and slavery because, hey, if nothing else, at least it was familiar. They were ready to walk away from the vision because it got too hard.

In the spacecraft, the astronauts faced a similar predicament. Now, unlike the Israelites, who still had the resources to complete their journey, these men did not. It was physically impossible for them to land on the moon and return to Earth. They had a choice. They could give in to their desperate situation. They could give in to that explosion and make peace with the lives they had lived before the oxygen ran out.

Or, they could give themselves a new mission—a new goal. Instead of aiming for the moon, they could aim to be safely back on Earth with their families. By refocusing the mission on survival, the men rediscovered that momentum, and between them and ground control, they did the impossible—they survived.

It's never easy to rally when things start going south. It requires so much energy to convince yourself to keep going, to keep looking ahead. You have to be a fighter when familiarity and comfort show up to drag you to complacency. It will inevitably be a tough match, but there are things you can do, questions you can ask, areas to which you can shift your attention to resist the pull of mediocrity.

First, remember why you can't stay "here." Addicts like Brandon have to reckon with the fact that if they stay, they will not survive. The people of Israel needed to remember the taskmasters' cruelty, the relentless, grueling lives of unending labor and misery they and generations before them had endured.

Second, remember where you're going! Think about how fantastic your destination is and how worthwhile it is for you to keep up the fight. The crew of Apollo 13—Jim Lovell, Fred Haise, and Jack Swigert—had to find a new "there" to aim for. While the moon was no longer an option, their children and wives were. They still had a reason to keep going.

These tactics are part of a five-part process of going from "here" to "there" that I call the Five Stages of a dream. Not one step or two steps. Five.

The astronauts of the moon missions made it into orbit on the Saturn V Rocket. It was the largest, most powerful craft ever created. It is designed in three stages, each one equally crucial to the mission's success, each one sequential and pivotal for the next. If you want to go from the Earth to the moon, you have to engage in all three stages.

If you want to move your life from "here" to "there," you must commit to each step of the process. Remember, no shortcuts.

CONCEPTION

What is your "there"?

This is where the dream is conceived. It's that idea you can't let go of, that unrelenting vision that keeps tugging at your heart. Just thinking about it fuels you, gets you out of bed every morning, and fills you with a greater sense of purpose.

Everything ever created by human hands started here. Someone had an embryonic epiphany of paper that would stick to stuff, and then, one day, Post-its arrived!

Someone thought that there must be a faster way to get things down on paper than a quill and ink. Years later, the printing press, later followed by typewriters, computers, your phone, and so on. It was all started somewhere by someone who dared to take the time to dream.

Walt Disney was a dreamer. His dedication to a mouse, good stories, and family fun have given the world everything you see right now on Disney Plus, not to mention Disneyland, Walt Disney World, and their counterparts around the globe. Walt's dreams gave us Space Mountain, Tomorrowland, and Olaf the Snowman.

Sadly, Walt died before the Magic Kingdom, now called Disney World, opened in Orlando, Florida. On the opening day of Disney World, someone remarked to creative director Mike Vance that it was too bad Walt Disney didn't live to see this day. Vance replied, "He did see it. That's why it's here."

What do you see? What idea or dream is percolating in your mind's eye? Are you ready to commit to it? If you want your dream to be more than a dream, decide today to make it a reality. You can do it but not without resolution, determination, and commitment.

CHALLENGES

You've now conceived your "there." It's real. It's still in your mind, but it's as real as you are willing to commit. Now, you need to determine what's between you and your goal. What obstacles do you have to overcome to reach "there"?

Pastor Tommy Barnett has achieved more than most could ever dream, with a list of accomplishments that could stretch for miles. One of his most outstanding achievements was founding the Dream Center in Los Angeles, California. The Dream Center has been pivotal in impacting the homelessness and drug crises in Los Angeles and has led to the opening of several Dream Centers all over the country.

I was lucky enough to have a conversation with him, and I asked him, "Knowing what you know now, if you could go back in time and tell a younger version of yourself one thing, what would it be?"

He did one of those deep-thinking stretches as he leaned back in his chair. It was almost like he was reaching back to his 12-year-old self. Then, as if hit with a lightning bolt, he sat up ramrod straight, looked me right in the eyes, and said, "I would dream bigger dreams and take bigger risks!"

Once he said that, I felt like I could take on the world, that no dream was out of reach. I hope you feel that way, too. However, many people aren't ready to assume the challenges that accompany those big dreams, which inherently come with bigger risks.

The word "risk" means exposure to danger. Your dreams may put your finances at risk. They may put your current career or professional standing on the line. They will almost inevitably put your free time, Netflix time, maybe even your family time at risk. While some of these things are not great sacrifices (you can let Netflix go), others are tremendously important and not ones you can treat flippantly or without regard. Family time is critically important—for your mental health and well-being and theirs. Does that mean everyone with a family should just stuff their dreams away in a closet? Absolutely not. It means that reaching your dreams will require additional problem-solving.

If you're starting a business, in addition to your business plan, construct a family plan. Write out a schedule that allows you time to be with those you love, time to experience fellowship and worship each week, and time to keep pressing ahead to your "there." Impossible simply means that you haven't found the solution yet, but if this is your "there," if this is the dream God has placed upon your heart, you will find a way.

CONNECTION IS CRUCIAL

Who do you want to go "there" with?

The exciting part of having a "there" is the joy of bringing others "there" with you. John Maxwell said: "Significance and selfishness are incompatible. Selfish people rarely find significance." He went on to say, "Success asks, 'How can I add value to myself?' Significance asks, 'How can I add value to others?'" and, "Once significance is sensed, nothing else will satisfy."[6]

Suppose you work hard and achieve your dream. When you get "there" all by yourself, have you been successful? Yes, but your success only applies to you. In this context, significance is having and achieving a dream so big that it impacts the lives of others and spurs them on to reach their own "there." You must keep in mind, though, that not everyone is called to the same "there." A wonderful pastor and expert on leadership, Rick Godwin, once said, "When you board a flight, they always give you a destination announcement. If you're not going there, you can get off. Leaders should frequently tell people where you're going, so the right people can get on and the wrong people can get off!"

Decide where you are going. Commit to doing what it takes to reach your destination. Remind yourself that you can't stay "here." Then give yourself and others a vision that is so compelling that you and they will risk everything to go from "here" to "there."

CHART YOUR COURSE

Where are you going?

The early astronauts had an exact destination—the moon—but getting there was infinitely more complex than just aiming for that big ball in the sky. First of all, Earth is continually moving. The moon

6   Maxwell, J. (2010). John Maxwell: Success or Significance. SUCCESS. Retrieved on December 18. 2020. Website: https://www.success.com/john-maxwell-success-or-significance/.

is also always moving, both at speeds of more than 25,000 mph. The slightest tweaks to the navigation system, the most delicate adjustments could have had them slamming into a lunar surface at unsurvivable speeds or skipping out of Earth's atmosphere into space, never to be seen again.

The numbers mattered, and the plans mattered. Not to mention, most of these numbers and figures were being worked out by hand. No graphing calculators or complicated computer programs were available yet. They were aiming for a moving target at mind-blowing speeds in an aircraft hardly anyone else had ever operated, but they did it. They did it because they were diligent and meticulous, and they planned for every eventuality and scenario. Then, when something unexpected happened, such as the Apollo 13 incident, they adjusted course, created new charts, and shifted their plans for their new goal—getting the astronauts home alive as soon as possible. They were able to adjust on the fly because they were so prepared, agile, and committed.

A lot of us have destinations in mind. We know where we want to go, but we haven't committed it to paper. We haven't mapped out each step between "here" and "there"; thus, we haven't gone anywhere because we haven't figured out how.

I once read the story about a team who set out to complete the "Three Peaks Challenge." Damien Davis and six friends set out to climb the United Kingdom's three highest mountains in memory of their friend, Wayne Wilson, who had died of leukemia.

Unfortunately, something went wrong in Scotland. Everything had seemed right. The maps seemed to align. However, when Mike, one of Damien's friends, reached the summit first, he had to make a heartbreaking announcement to his mates below.

"I hate to break this to you, sweetheart, but this ain't it."

They had climbed the wrong mountain.

Damien's response makes me laugh because I can hear myself saying something similar: "They all look the same from the bottom."

If you are charting a course or beginning to think about committing your dreams to a plan on paper, make sure to look up. Educate yourself. Know where you are and what you need to do to make it to where you want to go. Do you need to go back to school? Do you need to move across the country? Do you need to get out of a toxic relationship that is holding you back from your calling?

These are critically important questions to ask yourself and to continue to ask yourself along the way. As much work as you pour into a plan on the front end, it's not sacred. It's not etched in stone. More likely than not, it will need to change at some point along the way. Learn to be flexible—be prepared, but be agile.

Diligence and commitment are crucial to achieving any goal. Preparation and accommodation are just as critical. Just like the Earth and the Moon, you and your "there" are moving targets. The tiniest of adjustments will either land you where you want to be or shoot you off into space.

Always be aware of the thing that can alter your course. Other people, changes to a business, the stock market, your health, your family's health—countless factors can influence where you're going and how or if you'll get there. It's up to you to maintain your vigilance. Keep your eyes open, learn the navigation system, and keep your "there" in sight.

COMPLETION

Have a starting point and a finish line. How will you know when you get "there"?

Neil Armstrong and Buzz Aldrin had a pretty obvious answer to that question. When the supports of their Lunar Lander touched down, they knew they had arrived. They were finally "there"!

As he lowered himself rung by rung to the powdery lunar surface below, where no human foot had ever stood before, Armstrong spoke the immortal words that resonated around the world. "That's one small step for man. One giant leap for mankind."

He made it official. They had done it. They had gone from "here" to "there" and, by doing so, not only changed the course of human history but paved the way for others to return in their footsteps. They had a larger-than-life dream, and, through diligence, commitment, attention to the tiniest of details, and selfless sacrifice for a vision cast to an entire nation, they had made it.

Will your arrival be that clear? How will you know when your vision has been fulfilled? We went on vacation once to the Bahamas and had a layover in Georgia. I didn't get off the plane in Georgia, pull out my sunscreen, and start looking for the beach. Why? Because we weren't there yet! This was just a stop along the way. Our journey wasn't over.

It is critically important that you know exactly where it is that you are headed. Be specific. If your goal is to make it as a freelancer, but you don't establish a specific number of projects or amount of money you want to bring in over a specified period of time, how will you gauge your success? You can't! It's arbitrary and will either have you celebrating way too early or throwing in the towel along the way because it "feels" like you haven't accomplished anything.

"Feels" should have nothing to do with it. Have objective, concrete goals, and milestones. Chart out a schedule, create a network, a budget, or a to-do list. Hire yourself to be your own personal administrative assistant. That may sound tedious, but you will never know how close you are to "there" if you don't chart it. If you keep your goals vague, your days unstructured, and your time unallocated, a year from now, you will be in the exact same place.

Success takes planning. It requires action, and it hinges upon a stated, concrete goal or destination. What is your moon? What's your flight plan? Are you on a shuttle or a rocket? What will it take to get from "here" to "there"?

For Brandon, the first step to a new life was recognizing his "here." He had to acknowledge it and name it. "The very best step anybody can make is to admit that there's a problem. It was huge for me to be able to admit that I was an addict," he recalls.

His admission led to aspiration and the conception of an idea of a sober life. Just like the astronauts, he faced challenges, had to decide who would join him on his journey, had to make a plan, and had to chart a course. He did all of those things and saw his mission through to completion. He never took his eyes off his vision. He never let go of the hope of what might lie over "there." Today, Brandon is in full-time ministry, using his story, his experiences, his weaknesses, and his mistakes to help others discover Jesus, rediscover themselves, and begin their own journeys from "here" to "there."

Make a plan. Go through each of these stages, and take your dreams seriously. If you don't, no one else will. If you do legitimize your dreams, chart your course, equip yourself with the people and resources you will need along the way, establish an objective finish line and concrete progress trackers, the moon and back is just the beginning.

The Big Idea

Your current present was once your past
future, but now, you are "here."
So, what's next?
Do you have a "there"?
If you haven't begun your journey from "here"
to "there," what's holding you back?

Prayer

God, thank You for knowing every "here" and "there" in which I find myself. Help me learn what I need to learn on this journey. Give me Your eyes to see the vision You have waiting for me.

chapter 3

SEE 'N SAY
Breaking the Limit of Silence

Remember not the former things, nor consider the things of old.
Behold, I am doing a new thing now it springs forth, do you not
perceive it? I will make a way in the wilderness and rivers in the desert.
—Isaiah 43:18-19 (ESV)

I came to the conclusion that there is an existential
moment in your life when you must decide to speak
for yourself; nobody else can speak for you.
—Martin Luther King, Jr.[7]

When Dr. Martin Luther King, Jr., took to the podium on August 28, 1963, to address the 250,000 peaceful demonstrators marching in Washington, D.C., for full civil and economic rights for African Americans, no one, not even Dr. King, could have predicted the watershed moment they were about to experience.

---

7   King Jr., M. L. Accessed December 24, 2020, from goodreads.com. Website: https://www.
goodreads.com/quotes/731663-i-came-to-the-conclusion-that-there-is-an-existential.

The beginning of King's speech was not unlike many others he had given. He addressed historical injustices; he acknowledged the suffering many of those in attendance had experienced and encouraged them not to grow bitter.

He was eloquent and charismatic as always, but it had been a long day for everyone watching him. Restlessness was settling in, and there was somewhat of a lull in the energy between King and the crowd.

Ever attuned to the temperature of an audience, legendary gospel singer Mahalia Jackson, who was standing on the platform close to King, whispered in his ear, "Tell them about the dream."[8]

What came next changed history, but it wasn't the first time the dreams of one generation impacted another. In the earliest days of Christianity, following Jesus' death and resurrection, Peter and the other disciples gathered in one place. The Holy Spirit descended on them, enabling them to speak in many different languages.

Naturally, everyone around them was confused. Peter then spoke to the crowd and quoted what the prophet Joel had said in the Old Testament, as recounted in Acts 2:17 (NIV): "In the last days, God says I will pour out my Spirit on all people. Your sons and daughters will prophesy, your young men will see visions, your old men will dream dreams."

Essentially, Peter says that the younger men and women will prophesy or speak whatever they envision. These young people's visions emanate from the dreams of the generation before, meaning it is imperative never to stop dreaming. Dreams fuel vision; without

8   Jackson, M. Accessed December 24, 2020, from Bostonia. Website: https://www.bu.edu/bostonia/2013/mlk-i-have-a-dream-speech-50-year-anniversary/.

vision, there is nothing to say. When nothing is said, stagnation sets in. There is no growth, no change, no journey from "here" to "there."

When Dr. King was prompted to tell them about his dream, he accelerated one of the most critical milestones in modern history. He told the crowd of his dream to see white children and black children playing together. He spoke of a world in which sons of former slaves and sons of former slave owners could "sit at the table of brotherhood," a world in which his children would not be judged "by the color of their skin, but the content of their character."

With each statement, he became more than a speaker giving a speech. He became a visionary, inviting an entire generation to open its eyes and hearts to a dream of freedom, hope, and possibility. As he did so, the humanity of the crowd before him became increasingly apparent. The people weren't just demonstrators hoping for policy change. They were mothers, fathers, sons, and daughters who had been shunned, had watched their children shamed, had suffered an injury or even the death of a loved one due to their skin color. Every detail of his nearly inconceivable dream gave a voice to the voiceless, purpose to the downtrodden and listless, and the hope of a better tomorrow—the hope that they would not stay "here" forever. By sharing his vision, he gave them a "there."

Years later, King's wife, Coretta Scott King, reflected on the magnitude of the "I Have a Dream" speech, sharing that, "At that moment it seemed as if the Kingdom of God appeared."[9]

His words did not fall on deaf ears; instead, they inspired action. Within a year, the Civil Rights Act was passed, followed by the Voting

---

9   King, C. S. *A Testament of Hope: The Essential Writings and Speeches of Martin Luther King Jr.* Edited by James Washington, p. 217.2.

Rights Act of 1965. Dr. King had seen the possibility of a just society. This speech helped those in attendance and those watching on television across the country visualize what could be. He had been a steward of the vision and skills God had given him and ultimately became one of the most significant catalysts in moving the country from the norm of segregation to the ideal of integration.

This address and the man who delivered it came alongside the tireless work of other freedom fighters and helped bring the country from "here" to "there." He had a dream, saw a vision of what could be, claimed it, and spoke it into being. If you and I are to bring about change in our own lives, we must do the same. You must dream God-sized dreams if you are ever going to have a God-sized vision. Then, you have to share it. Words without vision are empty, but a vision silenced by fear, self-doubt, or oppression will wither and fade.

If you're ready to change your life, or move from "here" to "there," then there's no time like the present. It's time to open your eyes, look around, look up, look within, look everywhere until you lock eyes on your vision. Then, despite everything that may interfere with your line of sight, make a decision right here and right now to not look away.

NOW I SEE IT

The YouTube generation will never appreciate Saturday morning cartoons quite like the children of the 80s. Back then, there was no Cartoon Network or Nickelodeon or DVR. If you slept through Saturday morning cartoons ... well, you just didn't sleep through Saturday morning cartoons.

There was something special, almost sacred, about padding down to the living room from my bedroom before the rest of the world woke up. There, with the TV and a bowl of cereal, I got to know the Transformers, He-Man, and Skeletor. Between their armor and my pajamas, we took on the world of bad guys once a week, together making the earth a better, safer place to live for all humankind. (We thought quite highly of ourselves.)

Of course, what happened between the shows themselves was just as entertaining and, often, more expensive—the commercials! They were like a sneak peek into a world of play that I was born to be a part of. When a commercial came on for a new toy or new character, it would take all of 30 seconds to reel me in and get me hooked.

Thundercats is a standout in my memory. The first time I saw them, I knew they had to be a part of my life or I a part of theirs. When I told my mom of this exciting discovery, she was very mom-like in her response, "But we already got you He-Man."

She just didn't understand. I had to have Thundercats. Ten minutes ago I didn't, since I'd never seen or heard of them before. But one commercial was enough for me to realize what had missing in my life. I just needed to lay eyes on it.

Few things in life have been quite as captivating as that Thunder-cats commercial was to my 8-year-old self. However, the principle has made repeat appearances throughout my life. Once I see something, I can go after it. Until then, chances are I won't be budging. It's not because I'm stubborn, but because I don't know that there's another place I could be. That's how vision works. We typically don't leave "here" until God gives us a preview of "there." Once He does, however, our thoughts can be consumed with little else.

Famous athletes often tout the merit of vision in their preparation routines. Legendary golfer Jack Nicklaus even said that he never hit a single shot, even in practice, without having a sharp, clear image of it in his head. Michael Jordan would sit in the locker room before games and run through every play—every shot, rebound, dribble, or steal—and then he'd head to the court and make it happen. Both men—giants in their sports—knew that they were going nowhere without a vision of their destination.

Maybe acquiring such a vision is one of your biggest challenges. Perhaps inspiration hasn't struck, or you feel so locked into your immediate, day-to-day life and demands that you don't have time to breathe, much less dream about a great big someday.

I encourage you to rethink your position. History has proven over and over that it is impossible to spend time with a limitless God and maintain a small vision. This is the God who stretched out the giraffe's neck and painted stripes on zebras and tigers. It's the God who dotted the night sky with stars and planets and filled the dirt with hundreds of different insects who feed on hundreds of different plants and bacteria. There is no end to His masterpiece, and not only are you a part of it, but you can also take part in it. The more time you spend with God, the more He'll rub off on you. The more He rubs off on you, the more resistance you will face.

The devil doesn't attack small visions and half-hearted dreams. When Joshua and the men surrounded Jericho, Joshua knew that God had already given them the victory. He believed so strongly in the miracles that God was placing in their laps, he refused to see or couldn't see the potential problems. His view of God's promise of faithfulness was so bright it blinded him to doubt, second-guessing, and backtracking.

That's nice, you might be thinking. *Good for Joshua. I'm not there.*

You know what? That's ok, too. You're not alone, and you're not marooned in some stagnant holding chamber. You're not the only one who struggles to see the promise—whose grasp on big dreams is elusive. You may have heard the story of the little boy who walked along the beach where thousands of starfish had washed ashore. One by one, he picked them up and flung them back into the life-saving water. A man noticed what he was doing and asked him if he thought he could make any difference to all these starfish. The boy simply picked up another starfish, flung it back to the waves, and said, "It made a difference to that one."

Don't ever doubt your capacity to do great things. Don't limit your dreams because you feel inadequate or that your contribution would be negligible and, thus, not worth your time or effort. You will encounter people who will be skeptics, just like the man on the beach, but your role is not that of the cynic but that of the change-agent. Instead of starfish, pick up a word from God and share it with someone. Scripture says the Word does not return void. You put it out there. God will take over from there, and we've already established God doesn't do anything halfway. Throw your starfish, and watch what God will do.

Your dreams matter. You never age into obscurity or irrelevance unless you allow yourself to do so. Your dreams will fuel others' visions, and the bigger your dream, the bigger their visions will be.

Ask yourself what you want your community to look like in five years. Where do you want your children to be? What do you want to be doing? Resist the temptation to believe that God is done with you. Don't let your vision be blurred by age, professional status, relationships, or past failures.

Not long ago, I had LASIK surgery to correct a host of issues that were blurring my vision. Throughout the procedure, the doctor told me to keep looking at the light above my chair. "Stare at the light, Eric. Don't look away. Keep staring at the light. Don't lose your focus." Soon enough, he was done. My vision was completely restored.

When your vision starts to blur, focus on the light. Don't look away from Jesus. His glory is consuming, pushing trials, losses, and other challenges to the periphery. As you zero in on His face, you will see grace instead of shame. You will see blessing instead of bondage. His face radiates unconditional love, acceptance, and grace, obscuring our view of brokenness, poverty, anxiety, depression, or disease.

When I look at Jesus, I see glory and joy overflowing. When I look at Jesus, I see healing. When I look at Jesus, I see possibility and responsibility. If you are or I am truly committed to going the distance from "here" to "there," it's not enough for just our eyes to be open; our mouths should follow suit. What we say or don't say and how we say it will make the difference between progress and stagnation.

TIME TO SPEAK

In his lifetime, Dr. Martin Luther King, Jr., delivered over 2,500 speeches, authored six books, and wrote countless sermons. In 1964, at age 35, he became the youngest person to receive the Nobel Peace Prize for his non-violent leadership of the Civil Rights movement.

He was also arrested 29 times, his home and family endured many acts of violence, and he survived an assassination attempt 10 years before his death at the hand of a sniper. Every movement he led or speech he delivered put him in danger, yet he continued to take that risk, knowing that his words could create change.

In his autobiography, Dr. King wrote, "I came to the conclusion that there is an existential moment in your life when you must decide to speak for yourself; nobody else can speak for you."[10]

Ecclesiastes 3:7b (NIV) states that there is "a time to be silent, and a time to speak." The Bible never promises that those who speak up will be protected. It never even says that others will listen or seem to care. What it does say is that the words of God, once spoken, will not be for nothing. Isaiah 55:11 (ESV) states that His word "shall not return to me empty, but it shall accomplish that which I purpose, and shall succeed in the thing for which I sent it."

If you ever need evidence of a God-empowered voice, look no further than Joshua and the people of Israel surrounding the walls of Jericho. After 40 years of desert wandering, the people had finally reached the Promised Land, only to be met with imposing walls and a seemingly unconquerable army.

---

10 King Jr., M. L. Retrieved on December 24, 2020, from goodreads.com. Website: https://www.goodreads.com/quotes/731663-i-came-to-the-conclusion-that-there-is-an-existential.

However, God had not sent Moses to Pharaoh all those years ago to lead his people to a dead end. God knew about the walls that would await the Israelites, and He had a God-sized plan for bringing them down.

With great precision, God gave Joshua detailed instructions to ultimately take the city of Jericho. Joshua and his men were supposed to march around the city for six days. On the seventh, they were to blow their trumpets, should out loud, and let God do the rest.

And the scripture reads, "When the trumpets sounded, the army shouted, and at the sound of the trumpet when the men gave a loud shout, the wall collapsed; so everyone charged straight in, and they took the city" (Joshua 6:20, NIV).

Joshua listened to the words of God. The men listened to Joshua relay those words. Then, at the right time—God's time—they shouted, and the walls came down.

God had not weaponized their voices. He simply told them when and how to use them. He also told them how not to use them. As they were marching, they were told to stay silent. They neither talked about their day, nor commented on the scenery. They were to remain silent. Why? Because God knew that once they got close to the base of those walls and they started looking up at how big they were, somebody would say, "How do you think we're going to bring these walls down?"

Words hold great power. When you start facing walls, be careful who you're listening to and what you're saying to others and yourself. Proverbs 13:3 (ESV) says, "Whoever guards his mouth preserves his life; he who opens wide his lips comes to ruin." In other words, what comes out of your mouth will either help you conquer the foe in your path or lead you to surrender. When you think the wall you face is too big, your words can fortify it.

I can't do this. I don't think I can be healed from this. I don't believe God can give me a new job. I don't know if there are job openings right now. I don't have the right education.

Do you know what you're doing? You're giving strength to your walls. You are fortifying the barriers between "here" and "there." As damaging as self-talk can be, what you say to others can be equally uplifting or detrimental. Before you speak—to yourself or others, verbally or online—ask yourself five questions.

Are my words true?
Are they helpful?
Are they inspiring?
Are they necessary?
Are they kind?

Watch what you say. You get what you say, not what you want. Your words are seeds. Whatever you sow into your future, you will reap. Never underestimate your mouth's ability to influence your circumstances. Your mouth can change your world. In James 3, James writes that the tongue is like a rudder on a ship or a bit in an animal's mouth. It's small, but it can control the direction of the entire vessel or body.

BEFORE YOU SAY, "I DO"

I've married lots of couples. The routine is pretty much the same at each wedding:

I bring the bride and groom to the front.

I look at him and say, "Do you?" And he says, "I do."

I look at her, and I say, "Do you?" She says, "I do."

I bring them together in agreement. Their words bring them together in covenant. They come into contract on paper. They come into covenant with their mouths. They use the words to join together in covenant—not just between the two of them, but between them and God. And God makes a record of that.

Who or what are you standing at the altar with today and marrying your life to with your mouth? Some marry sickness or poverty. Some marry depression because one day, they said out loud that they agreed with depression. Jesus says when two or three agree on anything good or bad, that agreement will happen in your life. You may be in agreement with somebody or something that is holding your entire destiny back.

The moment you open your mouth and start that same old tape recorder—I'm not good enough, I'll never make it, etc.—you are inviting deceit into your mind and heart. You are disqualifying yourself from a limitless life.

When you speak the facts about your circumstances out loud, all you have are facts. And, facts remain facts until the truth shows up. There was a day when people said, "If you sail too far, you're going to fall off the edge of the earth because the earth is flat."

When Dr. King spoke of his dream in Washington, the facts at the time were that many restaurants, businesses, public transportation systems, even water fountains were separated—designated for black people and white people. Those were the facts. His vision was bigger than the facts. When he gave life and voice to the future he imagined, he helped propel a movement that would change those facts.

Whatever facts you are facing at this very moment, remember that God is bigger than your circumstances. Look for Him among the thorns entangling you today. What you see shapes and informs what you say. What you say shapes and informs your life.

When I was a little boy, I would take my dad's briefcase into church every Sunday before he would preach the sermon. There was a gentleman who would stop me and ask if I was going to preach that day. I would always say, "No, I'm not going to preach today."

Years later, it's my briefcase and the pulpit that God has given me the blessing to use for His glory. That man spoke over my life. And there are probably people speaking over the lives of you and your children right now.

There are some, maybe even you, who have no one to speak over them. When David went to kill Goliath, there was no one cheering him on. He didn't have any affirmations or even well wishes. Therefore, he spoke over himself.

He told himself he had killed bears and lions in defense of his sheep. He told himself, with God's help, he would kill the giant. He did.

Even if the world around you is silent, your future depends on your capacity to see your vision and speak it into existence. No one can believe it for you. At the end of the day, if you are stuck, struggling to see tomorrow, to see anything that you even want to talk about, remember that you weren't created to be stagnant. God wants you to move. He wants you to reach your "there," not because He is disappointed in you or because you need to snap out of it and just move on.

He wants you to leave "here" because He loves you so much, and His heart aches for your life to be full of the joy that awaits you "there."

If you are to make the journey from "here" to "there," it's time to open your eyes, see where you're going, and make your own proclamation to yourself and the rest of the world. Tell them about your dream!

See it. Say it. And with God's help, live in the fullness of the limitless life for which you were created.

The Big Idea

What you see is what you'll say. What you say is what you'll get. Are you paying attention to the words you are speaking?

Prayer

Father, I want to move from "here" to "there." I want to see You and the plan You have for me. Guide my eyes. Train my ears to hear Your voice. I surrender my words to Your will. Make them instruments of peace and weapons of grace.

chapter 4

FLUX CAPACITY

Breaking the Limit of Playing it Safe

*His master said to him, "Well done, good and faithful
servant. You have been faithful over a little; I will set
you over much. Enter into the joy of your master."*
—Matthew 25:21(ESV)

*The widest thing in the universe is not space; it is the potential
capacity of the human heart. Being made in the image of God,
it is capable of almost unlimited extension in all directions.*
—A. W. Tozer[11]

I t was 95 degrees. You could cut the humidity with a knife. Venturing outdoors in weather like that was usually the last thing on my to-do list. To go for a run in such conditions seemed like torture. I wasn't a runner.

Period.

---

11 Tozer, A. W. The Root of the Righteous. (1957). Retrieved from: https://www.goodreads. com/work/quotes/683975-the-root-of-the-righteous-tapping-the-bedrock-of-true-spirituality#:~:text="The%20widest%20thing%20in%20the,unlimited%20extension%20in%20 all%20directions., accessed October 7, 2020.

I don't run. Not even to the bathroom.

I was quite content on my couch or in a rocking chair, holding my son while observing that mysterious world of recreational runners from a comfortable, if somewhat complacent, distance.

"I bet that's nice," I would say to myself, "but I could never do that."

Unfortunately (so it seemed), I now had no choice but to become an asphalt-pounder. That very day, I had asked my congregation to be my accountability partner. I had promised that I would run a marathon in the next five years—I was convicted by my own sermon, and now I had a deadline.

So, I grabbed my headphones and left the comfort of my air-conditioned home to defy my "indoorsy" lifestyle. I walked for two minutes, jogged for three, walked for two, and attempted to jog for another three.

I thought I was going to die, praying that my Apple watch would hold out long enough for my wife to find me on the side of the road and begin resuscitation. Fortunately, I survived, and while day one of this new-found obligatory hobby was, to put it mildly, tough, I managed to survive day two. And day three. And many more.

I was light years away from the cover of Runner's World, but I had taken a step, albeit a small one, to increase my capacity. I had decided to take a risk on that sweltering hot day to deviate from my sedentary past and take action to enhance my future.

Feeling creative and inspired, I gave a name to this process—flux capacity. Shortly after that, feeling slightly less creative but no less insightful, I discovered that this was already a thing! With a definition and all. According to *Urban Dictionary*, flux capacity is "your ability to take action in the present to positively impact your future."[12]

Like me, if you are a fan of modern cinematic masterpieces, you can't hear the words "flux" or "future" without images of Marty McFly, Doc Brown, and that DeLorean time machine popping into your mind. *Back to the Future* is a timeless classic, introducing countless quotes into the modern-day lexicon and items that are nothing less than pop-cultural icons. Perhaps the most well-known is that odd device that powered the whole thing—the flux capacitor.

When Marty reached 88 miles per hour, the flux capacitor would take him to the timestamp of his choosing. The flux capacitor fueled the impossible. It stands to reason, therefore, that our own degree of flux capacity—our willingness to do something despite risk or discomfort—will either empower or derail our own "impossible." It determines whether we stay on that rocking chair looking out the window at others who appear to have blessings of strength and stamina, or we grab our running shoes and get outside.

RISKS, FEARS, AND FAITH

Matthew 25 contains a parable with some of the boldest assertions about God's take on passivity versus risk-taking and their direct impact upon blessings. Remember, a parable is an earthly illustration of a heavenly truth.

In this story, Jesus compares the kingdom of heaven to a man traveling to a far country. Before he leaves, he calls his servants together

---

12 Urban Dictionary, definition of "flux capacity." Retrieved on October 6, 2020, from Urban Dictionary. Website: https://www.urbandictionary.com/define.php?term=Flux%20capacity.

to distribute his goods among them. Referred to as "talents" in the scriptural text, "To one he gave five talents, to another two, to another one, to each according to his ability" (Matthew 25:15, ESV).

"Ability" is the key word here—I read that to be capacity. Each man received what his capacity would allow. As you read on, the logic behind the amount given to each servant becomes quite evident.

"He who had received the five talents went at once and traded with them, and he made five talents more. So also he who had the two talents made two talents more. But he who had received the one talent went and dug in the ground and hid his master's money" (vv. 17-18, ESV).

When the man returned from his journey, the homecoming went about as well as one would expect.

"And he who had received the five talents came forward, bringing five talents more, saying, 'Master, you delivered to me five talents; here, I have made five talents more.' His master said to him, 'Well done, good and faithful servant. You have been faithful over a little; I will set you over much. Enter into the joy of your master'" (vv. 20-21, ESV).

The story repeats with the servant who received two. He gained two more. And here, we take a left turn, as the man who received a single talent returned said talent upon retrieving it from the hole in which he had buried it.

The master replied: "You wicked and slothful servant! You knew that I reap where I have not sown and gather where I scattered no seed? Then you ought to have invested my money with the bankers, and at my coming, I should have received what was my own with interest" (vv. 26-27, ESV).

That seems pretty harsh. Add to it, the man took away the single talent from the docile servant, gave it to the go-getter with the ten, and then cast out the now-bankrupt servant "into the outer darkness. In that place there will be weeping and gnashing of teeth" (v. 30, ESV).

The man who had the least to risk risked the least and lost the most. He did nothing and lost everything. Unfair? Hardly. Not when you consider the master distributed the talents according to each person's abilities. Each of them had the potential to increase, but not all had the same capacity. While two men believed in the future of their possibilities, the other trusted his fear. By deciding that his future had no chance of changing or improving, he effectively eliminated every opportunity for growth and success. He turned down blessings before they even had the opportunity to be given.

FLIPPING YOUR PYRAMID

Do you remember when you were young, and anything in the world seemed to be possible? As a kid, you could see yourself as President of the United States, a gold medalist, or an astronaut. You were living life at the base of an inverted pyramid, with hopes and dreams as far and high as you could imagine. You entertained questions: *What do you want to be? What do you want to do? Where do you want to go? What languages do you want to speak?*

At that stage of life, anything is possible, primarily because you have not yet told yourself otherwise. You're starting small, but you have the opportunity to do whatever you want. You want to be a millionaire? It's up to you. The same is true for becoming a rocket scientist. A chemist. An inventor. A professor. An entrepreneur. A salesperson. A nurse. A forest ranger. A mechanic. It's up to you.

Let's say you have a sibling standing alongside you at the base of your pyramid. You are raised in the same family by the same parents, and you attend the same schools. Yet one of you goes on to become the astronaut or successful entrepreneur, while the other … well, not so much. You both had potential, and the capacity, but only one of you achieved success.

Why? Because somewhere along the way, someone or something flipped your inverted pyramid right side up. You haven't budged, yet you have convinced yourself that all the potential that was ahead of you is now behind you. That is simply not true.

Whether you are 25, 45, 65, or older, your potential has never changed. Your capacity has dwindled. If you do not see the likelihood of success, you may be living too small of a life. You have curtailed your choices, shut down your options, and limited your possibilities. Whether that has happened through other people, culture, or past disappointments, you've allowed the enemy to shrink your capacity.

Consider a baby just learning to talk. As the parent of a two year old, there's nothing I love more than listening to him try to form his first sentences. It's not perfect, but I understand him. He's speaking my language—English. But what if he was raised in another family that spoke a different language? Would he spend the rest of his life confused, not knowing what he heard? No, because as a two year old, he has the capacity to learn the language of his surrounding environment.

What about you? You might say, "I could never learn a new language. I'm too old for that now." Is that an issue of age or capacity? I believe that you could start now and become fluent in a new language in about five years. You can do a lot in five years.

Not only could you master all that Rosetta Stone has to offer, but you could also get a degree, learn a new skill, or master a sport. You could even be jumping out of airplanes on your own in the next five years. In five years, you could have enough home equity to sell and make a profit. You could read 60 books in five years. Given that the average book is about 200 pages, you would only have to read six pages per day. How long does it take to read six pages? Five minutes. You could also radically transform your soul and grow closer to God than ever before. By only reading two chapters of the Bible a day, you could read through God's Word three times in five years. You could do so much in five years.

The key is you have to do something. I frequently hear people woefully say things like, "I don't know if I'm helping anybody."

"I don't know that I have that much ability."

"Well, Pastor, I just retired."

Each statement like this indicates that at some point, these men and women flipped their pyramids and are convinced that their potential is behind them. They set limits in various arenas of their lives, and by doing so, they limited their capacity.

The solution? Flip the pyramid again! Go back to the beginning when potential and opportunity were wide open. Enlarge your world, be faithful with what you have at this moment, and prepare for God to bless you.

It's practically modern-day gospel to live or think "outside the box." While it's always important to expand your horizons and pursue creativity, too often, we presume that what is within our box is inadequate. So, rather than lamenting everything you don't have within your sphere of life and influence, thank God for what is in your box. Use it. Make the most of it.

We live in an age of zero excuses. You can't complain about not getting an education when you have four dozen books you haven't touched in years on your bookshelf at home. In the era of YouTube, you can't whine about not having access to special training. School may be financially out of reach, but just about every how-to under the sun is free of charge, courtesy of influencers and experts available 24 hours a day online.

You must flip your pyramid, trust in your potential, and stop limiting what God wants to still do in and through you.

INCREASE YOUR CAPACITY

As a leader, I would be doing a disservice to those around me, myself, and most importantly, to God, if I limited His blessings because I was too reticent to increase my capacity. That same logic goes for you, whether or not you are in a leadership role. Flux capacity originates with action. Yours will never grow if you are sedentary or complacent—no matter how comfortable stagnation may seem.

Like many others, I have often been faithful over nothing in my life. It's easy. I show up, I behave, and I follow all the rules. And yet, I do nothing. Let's be honest—God didn't save you or me to come here and sit in this auditorium every week. His definition of faithful is not doing nothing. God saved you to take the gifts He's put inside of you and use them to minister to others. We were not saved to sit. We have been saved to get—get going, get moving—and do something.

Like the three men in the parable, we have all been given a talent. Like these men, that talent isn't money—it's opportunity. Some people may have been given more opportunities. Some people may have been given one opportunity. Regardless of how many opportunities you have been given, what you do with them makes all the difference. Your behavior will determine whether your opportunity will grow or diminish.

Many of us have probably prayed for God to give us more opportunities. His response may very well have been, "I've already placed one in your hand, and you're not doing anything with it. You don't have the capacity for more." You may then wonder, *What is it about me that is limiting my capacity? What is keeping me from becoming all God wants me to be?*

The answer may be right in front of you, and it may be difficult to hear. If you spend your life blaming others for all that you lack, you are your own limitation—not them. The two faithful servants didn't let the lazy one impact them. His inaction had no impact upon their determination to multiply their opportunity. At the same time, the man who buried his opportunity in the ground did that all on his own. He can pin the blame on no one.

What's the difference between the men? Two had capacity while the other did not. A person with capacity will see 10 opportunities in a situation where the average person sees one. So, just what is capacity? I love defining it as "the maximum amount that something can contain and the amount that something can produce." You can only produce what you have received. If you are not producing a lot, it's because you have not received a lot. If you are not receiving a lot, it's because you don't have much capacity. People with capacity can receive and give on the same level.

Visualize a Dixie cup, a coffee mug, and a bucket ready to receive water from a giant pitcher. All can hold water, but when I pour water into the Dixie cup, it barely makes a dent in the pitcher because it doesn't have much capacity. The coffee mug takes a little more, but I can drain the pitcher when I move over to the bucket.

I see lots of Dixie-cup people always blaming God for why they don't have more in life. They run around, wearing their stress as a badge of honor and a convenient excuse to turn down opportunity. They have demanding jobs and just don't have time to come to church, or pay attention to their kids, or for anything else. They wonder why God seems to be blessing other people more than them but fail to realize that the pitcher is not to blame. It can only pour what they can receive.

Then there are the bucket people. They travel four days a week and still manage to raise children, volunteer in their off hours, invest in community initiatives, and show up early Sunday to help at church. The difference? Capacity. If God gave a Dixie-cup person what He's given to the bucket person, it might crush him or her. That person could give up on faith, walk out of church, and turn back to old habits—all the while bemoaning why God put so much on them, yet asking for more at the same time.

Think about this from a parent's perspective. When my daughter, Saige, asks for a puppy, I have to say, "I would consider it if you would just clean your room. But if you can't keep your room clean now, how could you help keep the house clean with a dog in it?"

What if you were praying for a new car because yours has 250,000 miles on it, needs constant maintenance, and may or may not start acting up depending on the temperature outside. You're desperate, but it's more than the inner mechanics that are problematic. It looks like a wreck. It hasn't been vacuumed in three years, still has sand on the floor from your last visit to the beach, and has McDonald's wrappers and stiff French fries scattered around the back seat. What makes you think that God will entrust you with more? People love to say, "God will never put more on me than I can bear," but that can work both ways—positively or negatively. He's not going to give you more blessing than you can handle, either.

So, how do you get more blessings? Increase your capacity. If you want a coffee-cup blessing, you have to move beyond Dixie-cup thinking. And if you want bucket-level blessings, you're going to have to get out of living in a coffee-cup mindset. Realize, though, that you can't do this through your own strength. This type of growth requires the power of the Holy Spirit. Pray to God and ask Him to help you increase. Start surrounding yourself with people who have greater capacity too. Observe how they handle things, and learn from them. As your capacity grows, God will trust you with more.

To be clear, you shouldn't want more for the sake of having more. God blesses us to bless others, not so we can kick back and take it easy. Once you reach the stage of complacency, God will say, "You can't handle anymore. You're already full." When we're full and comfortable and stop seeking expansion, God stops pouring—anointing, favor, provision, or opportunities.

Acquiring opportunities is only half the battle. Once you have a possibility before you, you have to step into it. How? First, you have to shut the door on fear of failure. Fear led that servant straight to a shovel and a hole. Don't allow your fear to shut you down. Chances are, you may very well try and fail, but so what? You learn something and go back and try again. Each risk you take stretches your capacity more and more. Besides, God likes risky people.

When a man like Gideon walks out and says, "Yeah, I'll take on an army of a thousand guys," God's like, "This is going to be fun." When a young man like David says, "Yeah, I'll fight that giant," and someone says, "You don't have a sword," he replies, "That's okay. I've got a slingshot." When Peter says, "I'll walk on water," Jesus tells him to come. God enjoys people who put it all on the line.

At times, that behavior may seem counterintuitive. The servant who buried the talent appears to be wise, prudent, and careful. He feared potential punishment from his master if he were to lose a single penny.

Oddly enough, all three servants served the same master but had wildly different perceptions of him. Likewise, not all Christians perceive God in the same way. Oftentimes, we tend to find what we're looking for. Looking for the goodness of God? You'll find it. Looking for the anger and judgment of God? You'll find it, too. I believe in looking for the goodness of God. He's not out to get you or find reasons to punish you, but rather He's looking for an excuse to bless you. He's waiting for you to increase your capacity, so He can give you more.

Two birds exist in the desert—a vulture and a hummingbird. They are distinctly different birds, as the vulture lives on dead things while the hummingbird survives on the sweet nectar from cactus flowers. In the vast, arid desert landscape, both find what they are looking for. The vulture looks for death and finds it, while the hummingbird seeks out and finds life. Whatever it is that you are looking for today, chances are, you'll find it.

GET COMFORTABLE
BEING UNCOMFORTABLE

While you look for the goodness of God, remember this big idea: We control our capacities. There are things in life that you have no control over. You can't control the family you're born into or what has happened in the past. However, your capacity is not predetermined; you can choose to increase it. One way to do this is to identify your lids. These are the barriers you have erected in your life to constrain your capacity, and everyone has them. They might be the way you think, the words you speak, or the people you hang out with. If you surround yourself with small-minded people, it's likely that you, too, will be small-minded. The reverse is also true. When Henry Ford invented the assembly line, he said, "I'm looking for a lot of men with an infinite capacity for not knowing what can't be done."

Fair warning. Once you begin removing these lids, venturing beyond the barriers you've come to know, prepare to feel uncomfortable. The degree to which you stretch your capacity is determined by your tolerance for pain. Proverbs 24:10 (ESV) says, "If you faint in the day of adversity, your strength is small." When the pressure starts hitting your life, if you start falling apart, your strength is small. The amount of pain you can withstand is equivalent to your strength and capacity.

Think about every mother who has gone through pregnancy and brought life into this world. What her body goes through is a miracle—beautiful and horrific all at the same time. During pregnancy, it is amazing how bones and skin will start stretching out of place. Some organs will even begin moving around to accommodate the baby. And that's just what happens during pregnancy. From the moment of conception, a woman's body must increase its capacity to support the life inside.

The same thing happens to us spiritually. What is God trying to move in your life that you don't want Him to? God may say, "Unless I move this, I can't expand your capacity. What I'm trying to birth out of you will die in the womb unless you let me move this, stretch this, or rearrange this."

The pushing and prodding will likely be painful. Let's revisit my running endeavor. On that very first run, I could barely keep going for more than two minutes at a time, but after about four weeks, I ran 36 minutes straight. I was with a friend, and we kept running until we hit three miles. I'm believing that each of those 36 minutes is a down payment on the 27 miles that I'm going to run in that marathon. Was it easy to reach this point? Good Lord, no! But guess what? Three miles was always in me. I just kept denying it because I didn't want to stretch my capacity. The process was painful, but the promotion was awesome. Looking back, I kept thinking, "Oh, my goodness. Why didn't I do this sooner?"

Let's revisit the three men once more. The first man never looked at the master to say, "Hey, since I did so well, can you reward me?" It's not in the scripture, but here's what it shows us. The blessing is triggered by capacity. When you increase your capacity, you don't even have to pray for God to bless you. When you increase your capacity, God will send more just because He knows you can handle it. They didn't have to ask for more; their capacities demanded more. Let me ask you this question: *Is your capacity putting a demand on God today?*

BENEATH THE SURFACE

In his book, *The Root of the Righteous*, noted Pastor A. W. Tozer wrote, "The widest thing in the universe is not space; it is the potential capacity of the human heart. Being made in the image of God, it is capable of almost unlimited extension in all directions. And one of the world's worst tragedies is that we allow our hearts to shrink until there is room in them for little beside ourselves."[13]

Those words inspire me, as does the story I read once about the Great Depression of the 1930s when unemployment rose to 25 percent and millions struggled to survive. E. L. Yates was one of them, eking out a living on his West Texas sheep farm, worrying about how to pay his bills and feed his family. Thoughts of filing bankruptcy and looking for a fresh start occupied his mind. However, before the bank could complete repossession proceedings, a survey crew from an oil

13 "The Root of the Righteous Quotes," Retrieved on October 7, 2020, from GoodReads, Website: goodreads.com/work/quotes/683975-the-root-of-the-righteous-tapping-the-bedrock-of-true-spirituality#:~:text="The%20widest%20thing%20in%20the,unlimited%20extension%20in%20 all%20directions.

company came and asked Yates for permission to search for oil on his land. They offered a contract stating he would receive a 12.5 percent royalty on any production.

The company soon hit a gusher that produced 80,000 barrels of oil a day. 30 years after Yates signed that deal, a government survey showed wells in the area with the capacity for 125,000 barrels a day. Yates's well kept going and, by the late 1990s, had produced more than one billion barrels of oil, with another billion in the ground. He was about to throw in the towel when the blessing was right under his feet.

What's beneath your surface? God wants to release something, but you have to increase your capacity to receive it. People who have capacity know what to do when opportunity shows up. They are prepared. They don't just wing it and expect to get ready the instant an opportunity shows up. They live lives of awareness and preparation, always priming and readying their flux capacity.

Don't allow your fear to shortchange your possibilities. The servant who lost it all did so, trying to protect what he was too afraid to lose. What he held so tightly was ultimately ripped away because he didn't have faith enough to take action, take risks, and trust in his own potential.

The Big Idea

God is with the risky. If you read the Word of God, it's almost as if there's an attraction between God and risky people. Whenever people put it all on the line, God just hangs around them.

What is holding you back today?

What lies beneath the surface, ready to be

tapped once your capacity has expanded?

Are you ready to step into more?

Prayer

I commit to enlarging my capacity for God, people, and life so that I can receive and be all that God intended for me to be.

chapter 5

DEFINING MOMENTS

Breaking the Limit of Apathy

"As for me and my house, we will serve the Lord."
—Joshua 24:15b (ESV)

*"I did not know, as I listened to Father's footsteps
winding back down the stairs, that he had given me
more than the key to this hard moment."*
—Corrie ten Boom[14]

The grocery bags were swinging from our wrists as we stepped out of Kroger. The trunk lid swung open at the same time that Kim's phone began to ring. I stood in the back of the car, putting in the milk and then the bread, careful not to crush the chips. I didn't have thoughts much further than dinner as I put the cart back into the rack. As I opened the car door, though, the look on Kim's face told me that our lives were about to change.

---

14 Corrie ten Boom (n.d.). Goodreads.com. Retrieved on December 13, 2020, from Goodreads.
com. Website: https://www.goodreads.com/work/quotes/878114-the-hiding-place.

Her tears etched an indelible image that will forever be in my mind. It has become a defining moment in both of our lives. That was when we learned the little girl growing in Kim's belly had cysts throughout her brain. The best-case scenario was survival—but she would likely be born with Down's Syndrome and have no quality of life. That's when the doctor said, "We need to talk about terminating the pregnancy."

I've gotten groceries countless times. I've watched my wife receive numerous phone calls. But that day—that phone call in that Kroger parking lot is the one that will stay with me forever. It was a defining moment.

A defining moment is a point in your life that fundamentally changes you. You made a decision, or you received a diagnosis, or you met someone, and it changed the course of your life from the inside out. It can happen to you as an individual, a couple, a family, even as a church.

The Bible is filled with defining moments. But one has perhaps no more significant impact upon generations than that at the end of Joshua's life. Now Joshua has no shortage of weighty moments. He has borne witness to some of the most extraordinary events in history and has stood at the right hand of Moses, the man who spoke with God face-to-face, delivered God's people from bondage, and received the Ten Commandments from the very finger of God.

These are the moments that have comprised Joshua's life. Yet, when it comes to his own words of wisdom, the moment when he would leave a generational imprint, there are none so impactful as the ones that came at the end of his life.

He knew the end was coming, so he gathered the elders, leaders, and captains of the children of Israel and told them he had something important to say. This wasn't just another announcement. Everything about this was momentous. From the location to the declarations to the life-altering decision he put before them at the end.

"Joshua gathered all the tribes of Israel to Shechem and summoned the elders, the heads, the judges, and the officers of Israel" (Joshua 24:1a, ESV). It was the location where both Abraham and Jacob camped and built altars when they stayed in the Promised Land for the first time, and it had been the backdrop for other significant events throughout the people's history. The attendees were an impressive group. These were the top leaders, and they were coming together in the conscious presence of God.

Then Joshua began to speak, and if you're at all familiar with this man, you know he's had some impressive oratory moments: "Have I not commanded you? Be strong and courageous. Do not be frightened, and do not be dismayed, for the Lord your God is with you wherever you go" (Joshua 1:9, ESV). And, after seven days of marching around Jericho, Joshua had declared to the people: "Shout, for the Lord has given you the city" (Joshua 6:16b, ESV).

These moments and words highlight an impressive life. But the speech Joshua launches into at this gathering is one that historically will overshadow everything he has said prior. This is his "I Have a Dream" moment. Why?

As he recounted God's faithfulness throughout the years, it was as though he was God's inspired messenger. He was delivering the history of God's chosen people, the accounts of the miraculous wonders that brought them from slavery to freedom, from conquered to conquerors, from the oppressed to the victors. Then he put before them a choice—in light of God's faithfulness, where would theirs reside? He spent his last moments laying out the gravity of this choice.

Joshua knew that we all would serve something. He wanted them to be aware that this decision mattered, so he made the declaration that has lived on—that has become the defining headline of his life: "As for me and my house, we will serve the Lord" (Joshua 24:15b, ESV).

Soon after, he would die. Yet, Joshua didn't let the gravity of this moment escape. He was at the end of his life; time itself was against him. Ultimately, he chose to take that moment captive. More often than not, defining moments happen when everything's against you. In those moments, you can let them define you, or you can define them. Joshua never allowed disappointment or failure to define his life. He defined it by the presence and promise of God.

KROGER IS SHECHEM

Kim and I didn't foresee our Kroger run as a defining moment. We had been walking on air. Finally, our Saige was on her way and, while I was more than a little worried that I wouldn't have what it took to pull off Barbies and tea parties (I know football!), I knew that a miracle was on her way who would change our lives forever. I just didn't think it would be like this.

As we digested the news of our unborn child's potentially devastating diagnosis, I did what any faith-filled leader of God would do: I reached out to everyone I knew. I called my parents, the church elders, and a friend. I only got voicemail. So then, I did the second thing a faith-filled leader of God would do: I remembered God. In retrospect, this should have been my first option, but eventually I remembered that "me and my house" served a God of miraculous healing.

Just a couple of years into our marriage, I began having headaches. These were not aspirin or Tylenol headaches. These were the most intense, painful things I had ever experienced. It was as though a hammer were pounding away—relentlessly and without regard.

I underwent a brain scan, an MRI, an MRA, and a host of other tests. Finally, when the doctor called, he said, "Are you sitting down?"

That's never good.

"Everything looks normal," he said. "There are no signs that you've ever had a migraine. However, your MRA came back, and it appears there's a blood vessel in the back of your brain, and it's blocked by 70 percent."

"What are our options?"

"You were born this way," he replied. "Unfortunately, there's nothing we can give you, and because of where it's located, there's no surgery we can do to take it out."

"So, what's going to happen?" I asked.

"One of two things. You'll either have an aneurysm, or you're going to have a stroke, and there's nothing we can do about either. We're going to send you to a specialist in downtown Cincinnati for further examination. He's one of the top neurologists in the nation."

That was a defining moment. With the words of Joshua 24:15 echoing in my head, at our next service, the church members gathered and prayed over me. When I returned for a follow-up scan, the doctor's nurse called with the results.

"This is Robin from Dr. Reed's office. We have your report back. The doctor's taken a look at it. We want to let you know that whatever was there isn't there anymore. Your brain is perfectly normal."

So, as I stood with Kim, my hand on her belly, I prayed, "Lord, if you can heal me, you can heal her."

It wasn't an easy prayer to pray, but it was the right prayer to pray. At the next ultrasound, the nurse said, "Wow! Whatever was there in your daughter's brain isn't there anymore. Your daughter's perfect."

She was right. It was a defining moment. Nothing has been the same since. Saige was born healthy and brilliant. She is the most outstanding daughter parents could ask for. How different would that seem, had we not experienced this earth-shattering moment? How much more do we appreciate and rejoice in the life that is our daughter's because we were so close to losing it? How did we have the faith to believe in God's healing? Because of the other defining moment on the other end of a call from a doctor. Time and time again, God had proven faithful. Time and time again, He had come through. Blocked arteries and brain cysts have not defined the headlines of our lives. They have been written by miraculous healing and redeeming grace.

MOUNTAINS AND VALLEYS

Reflecting upon my life, I can identify seismic, faith-fortifying miracles and moments. But I don't live life on miracles. I live my life between miracles. Goliath shows up in the valley, and Goliath says, "I'm your next problem." However, his presence tells me there's another miracle on the way. He's going to try to push back on me; he can't push me back any farther than my last miracle, because when I look back at what God's done in my life, I can't go back. I won't go back. I will serve the Lord.

The trick is remembering God's provision in the middle of a dip. When you are first saved, you are having your wilderness experience. God is getting you out of Egypt and getting Egypt out of you. How? He provides for you. You may be out of toothpaste and pray for toothpaste, and samples of Crest show up in your mailbox. Or you pray for a parking spot, and one is reserved for you in the front.

Everything is good! Just like He did for the people of Israel—Joshua's people—He is providing manna and quail for you. Then things change. Scripture tells us that once the people reached the Promised Land, the manna and quail stopped coming. Maybe you don't get the job, or you get the call from the doctor.

This is the area that has been referred to as the crisis of belief. In other words, what I see doesn't line up with what I believe. I believe God is a healer, but the doctor just said I have cancer. I believe He's my provider, but I just lost the job, and I can't pay the bills.

This is the *valley*. How long you stay in this valley is up to you. The valley is all about getting you to decide your life. Valleys of decision lead to mountains of provision.

Who are you going to serve? Who are you going to trust? Are you going to trust what God was doing for you, or are you just going to trust God? Even when you can't see it and what you do see doesn't line up with what you believe, are you still going to trust God?

This is where Joshua shows up and says, "Make a decision." I think that Joshua's question deserves our consideration because it's coming from a man well-acquainted with hardship. Joshua had every right to play the victim. He was a slave in Egypt, he experienced the plagues and the Passover, and he was there when Pharaoh sent the slaves into the desert. That's when Joshua was no longer a slave; he became a servant.

By most standards, this is hardly a step-up. It's barely a lateral move. He'd been a slave his whole life and was now fetching water for Moses. The Bible tells us in Zechariah not to despise the day of small beginnings. What you are doing right now may not seem important. It may seem demeaning, but God put you there for a reason.

Joshua was serving the man chosen by God, who talks with Him face-to-face. He was in the company of one of the most legendary leaders in human history not because of a title but because of his service. Most of us will never see the private living quarters of the president or the Queen of England. But do you know who will? The maid. Because serving can get you into rooms that titles can't.

So, Joshua is serving. While he's serving, he's learning. When Moses dies, Joshua is ready to take his place. He is prepared to lead the people. Does he do it perfectly? Not anywhere close. He wasn't sensitive to the voice of God when he sent men from Ai to spy out the region. His poor decision making resulted in the deaths of 36 men. He made a covenant with God's enemies. He trusted in God's victory at Jericho when everyone else doubted. He wandered a desert for 40 years. He had a hard life, but when his back was against the wall, on his way out of this life, he makes a decision that defines his life and becomes his headline. He chooses to serve the Lord.

CHOOSE THIS DAY

When you are in a valley, you have two choices. The first is you can quit. You can go back to Egypt. God has delivered you from the bondage of addiction, selfishness, and conflict, but you can always go back to it. For most people, that's the easiest way to go. It's a hard place, a painful place, but it's familiar. We may incur scars, but we see them coming.

As you wrestle with this choice, you may be wondering why God doesn't just take you to the mountaintop. The answer is pretty straight-forward—He wants to see whether you will trust Him in the valley. Anyone can praise on the mountaintop. Mountaintops reveal character. Valleys reveal your faith.

Your second choice is to stand and fight. If there is one ounce of belief in you that believes in God's redeeming grace and power, then you can stand flat-footed, look the devil in the eye, and say, "I'm more determined than you are." When you do, you will come through the valley into a mountaintop of promise and reward more lavish than you could ever imagine.

When I graduated high school, a friend talked me into going to Bible college. After a semester or two, I panicked. I didn't want to stay. I wanted to go home and become a realtor or a banker. I told my mom such, and she responded, "Eric, just give it another month." During that month, I was filled with the Holy Spirit and received God's call to ministry. This was a miracle moment. It represents a crucial time when God filled me with hope and showed me my purpose for being on this earth—it was a defining moment.

I went home and began serving alongside my father in our church and was utterly fulfilled, knowing that I was living into my purpose.

Then, another valley crept in. I was lonely. I was particular with God when it came to my marriage criteria. I didn't want just a pretty woman. There are lots of lovely people out there. I wanted someone beautiful, smart, and intelligent. I wanted someone who would walk beside me—not behind me—in ministry. While I was praying all of this, though, I was the church's public relations director and knew I couldn't meet this miracle of mine in a club or a bar.

I said to God, "If you don't bring her to this church and walk her down the aisle, Lord, I'm never going to meet her." So, on a Wednesday night, God brought Kim to the church and walked her down the aisle. That's where we met.

Time and time again, God has come through. He met me in every valley; He comforted me in my times of indecision. He brought me to the mountaintops and gave me multitudes of blessings, which I have and still turn back to praise.

ME AND MY HOUSE

When the doctor told us to seriously consider aborting Saige, we had to choose. We had never been here before. As we stared into the darkness of a great unknown, we could have despaired, forgotten the promises and miracles of the past, and, quite possibly, terminated the life of our perfect little girl. That may sound dramatic. It is. That's how big of a deal this was.

We cannot live our lives so focused on what is in front of us that we forget what is behind us. We can't allow the fear of today to negate the miracles of yesterday. At the same time, we can't get so consumed by the past or present that we forget the next mountaintop is within reach. We must live where celebration and anticipation coexist. This is where the promise of God dwells.

Joshua shared a wealth of wisdom in his simple statement. He let us know that we always have the option of God. Always. It doesn't matter what's happening now, what has happened in the past, or what has yet to take place. God is always an option. What we do with that option will define who we become.

The Big Idea

The moment can define you, or you can define the moment.
If you are facing the impossible, have you taken the time to
reflect on other situations through which God has carried you?
Are you ready to choose right here, right
now, whom you will serve?

Prayer

*Lord, when these hardships enter my life, help me remember
that their presence is an indication of Your next miracle.
Help me take these moments captive and trust You and
Your provision. Help me define the moment and allow the
blessings, and not the hardships, to write my headlines.*

chapter 6

WITHIN REACH
Breaking the Limit of Inadequacy

*May the Lord, the God of your fathers, make you a thousand times
as many as you are and bless you, as he has promised you!*
—Deuteronomy 1:11(ESV)

*Be willing to transition at every stage of your life. If your heart
is open and you have an open mind, the blessing will flow.*
—T. D. Jakes[15]

If there is one thing that is constant in life, it is change. Transitions are the hallmark of human existence and the moments of faith that define who we become and the purpose we do or do not fulfill.

There are few historical figures whose lives were hallmarked by more change than Moses. He's a stand-out when it comes to Biblical heroes. His life was one of obedience, faithfulness, and redemption. Perhaps one of the most relatable features of Moses' life, however, was transition. He goes from one significant life change to another.

15 Jakes, T.D. Retrieved on January 3, 2021, from AwakenTheGreatnessWithin. Website: https://www.awakenthegreatnesswithin.com/25-inspirational-quotes-on-transition/.

Your life is probably similar. Just about the time you start to get comfortable in one arena, something changes, and you've got to find your bearings all over again. Maybe you were promoted, or demoted, or fired. Perhaps you got married and then had a baby. Maybe your baby is just now becoming mobile, and it is "All hands on deck!" 24 hours a day. Maybe you are now an empty nester or are mourning the loss of a loved one. You may have spent 20 years nurturing a marriage that is now over, or you've raised a child who has become a rebellious teenager.

Whatever curveball life is lobbing your way, it's thrown you off your game. You are no longer on a familiar path and must make adjustments to navigate this new road. These types of changes are life-altering and, most of all, inevitable.

Moses' life was hallmarked by transition. Precisely, his life unfolds in three acts, each of which lasts about 40 years. The first 40, he spent in the house of Pharaoh, a lauded Prince of Egypt. In his second 40, he herded sheep. In the latter 40, he led God's people to a Promised Land.

As disjointed as these three phases may appear, each is preparation for the next. Not a single year or experience was wasted. Forty years in the palace prepared him to deal with Pharoah. Forty years with the sheep prepared him to lead God's people.

Wherever you are right now, don't assume that this moment is wasted. God can use your present circumstances in ways that you can't even begin to fathom. The question is this: *Are you ready for more? Are you ready to take the next step? Are you prepared to step into something new—transition to a role that you never saw yourself taking on?*

If you are facing transition, consider the process through which Moses went. When he encountered the burning bush, God said to him, "Take off your sandals, for the place where you are standing is Holy ground" (Exodus 3:5, NIV).

The first thing that God speaks to Moses about is his feet. Whenever you come into a transition, the first thing that's going to change is your direction. You've been walking 40 years in this direction, but you're about to go in a new direction. You've lived your whole life this way, but after this encounter, you'll never be able to live that way again. God is going to change the way you walk. He is going to change where you walk, how you walk, and with whom you walk.

Then God lays it all on the line. He tells Moses that He has seen His people's suffering and is ready to bring them out of bondage and has chosen Moses for the job.

"I am sending you to Pharaoh to bring my people the Israelites out of Egypt" (Exodus 3:10b, NIV).

Enter the questions. At God's declaration over the role Moses would play in freeing the Israelites, Moses does what anyone would do: He asks questions.

WHO AM I?

Identity is a huge component of the transition. If you've ever lost a job or a spouse, it may be difficult to recognize who you are or the role you are intended to play from this point forward. Many people define themselves by their profession. Parents may define themselves by their children. When that job goes away, or those kids move out, we don't know who we are.

When God puts a promotion or a new task before us, it's tempting to measure ourselves with who we have been and, more often than not, attempt to disqualify ourselves before we've even begun.

Moses had murdered in Egypt. He had been kicked out of the house of Pharaoh. He was nothing but a shepherd now. Who was he to be God's great deliverer?

Unsurprisingly, God had an answer. Moses was placed in a basket on the Nile River as a baby, discovered by Pharaoh's daughter, and raised in Egypt's most outstanding schools. He learned the strengths and weaknesses of every god that was worshiped within the kingdom of Egypt. He knew how to build like the Egyptians, talk like the Egyptians, dress like the Egyptians, and think like the Egyptians. What better preparation for understanding your enemy than being raised among them? Perhaps you feel surrounded by enemies today because God teaches you about those whom you will one day overcome.

Moses' upbringing was a tutorial for a future assignment. Oddly enough, his downfall was as well. While still in Egypt, Moses committed murder and was banished to the desert, where he spent 40 years surrounded by sheep. He went from being waited on hand and foot to a desert with dirty sheep.

If you were to look at Moses' education and previous experience, you would deduce that he was vastly overqualified to be a shepherd. And there is nothing quite so humbling as taking a position for which you are overqualified, especially when your failure put you there.

Maybe you lost your temper at work and, despite having a degree in chemical engineering, you are serving coffee at Starbucks. When you go home with a dirty apron and stare at your degrees on your wall, you're going to want to ask, "Why?"

More likely than not, your present situation is teaching you a necessary lesson for a future opportunity. During Moses' second 40 years, he learned what it was to live with hurting people. He knew what it was to be without endless resources. His experiences would help him identify with those whom he would lead out of bondage. It's challenging to guide those with whom you can't identify or whose circumstances you don't understand.

There is a reason I can effectively minister to people who struggle with anxiety. I've walked through that valley, and God has brought me through. Therefore, I can more effectively minister to people dealing with the same thing because I'm not just talking to them; I'm walking with them.

Whatever it is you are walking through or have walked through, nothing is wasted. I'm talking to the parents whose kid is strung out on drugs. No experience is ever wasted. I'm talking to the man who just got laid off from work, and you don't know who you are anymore. No experience is ever wasted. God is teaching you something at this time. How long you stay there depends on how quickly you learn the lesson and are ready to pass the test and move on to the next level.

How long did it take Moses? After 80 years, he's ready to accept his calling. How long is it going to take you? Why don't you choose to accept who God says you are and do what He's asked you to do so you can move on and be all that He says you can be?

The truth is, Satan is not bothered by who you were. He couldn't care less. The devil's not even troubled by who you are right now.

What terrorizes Satan is who you can become; therefore, it is his goal to stop you while in transition.

Not everyone becomes who God has intended him or her to become because few people are ready to dig in and do the hard work that change requires. But, if you are to live fully in the role to which He has called you, prepare yourself for leaving what is familiar and venturing into the unknown.

WHO ARE YOU?

Moses' first question was about himself. His second was about the One who was calling him: "Then Moses said to God, 'If I come to the people of Israel and say to them, "The God of your fathers has sent me to you," and they ask me, "What is his name?" what shall I say to them?' God said to Moses, 'I AM who I AM.' And he said, 'Say this to the people of Israel: "I AM has sent me to you""' (Exodus 3:13-14, ESV).

If I were Moses, I'd probably have pressed for some more explanation. "You are ... what?" God doesn't give him a statement; He gives him half a sentence. Because God is so big, one name can't define Him. Who He is depends on the season in which you find yourself. When you are weak, He is *El Shaddai*, the Lord, God Almighty. When you need encouragement, He is *Jehovah-Nissi*, the Lord, my Banner. When you need direction, He is *Jehovah-Rohi*, the Lord, my Shepherd. When you need healing, He is *Jehovah-Rapha*, the Lord, my Healer. And when you feel alone—like nobody's there—He says, "Don't worry, I am *Jehovah-Shammah*. I am there. You need to know that I am there." When you feel like you're running out of energy or ability, He says, I am *Elohim*, the Everlasting God. I'll outlast every enemy in your life. When you don't have enough, He says, I am *Jehovah-Jireh*, your Provider. When you feel troubled in your spirit, and you're in a storm, He is *Jehovah-shalom*, your Peace that passes all understanding. Whatever you need, that's what He is.

Why is it so important to know who God is? Because you will never know who you are if you don't know who He is—not what someone has told you about Him—but first-hand knowledge of the character of God. If you find yourself in a storm and pray for the God of your grandmother to show up, the problem is that you don't know Him. You have to come to know Him for yourself. Only then will you honestly know who you are.

WHAT IF THEY DON'T BELIEVE ME?

In Exodus 4, Moses continued with his questions, asking the Lord what he should do if and when Pharaoh and those around him didn't believe or listen to him. God gave him a pretty fantastic response, telling him to throw his staff on the ground. He did, and it became a snake, which Moses then ran from before God told him to pick it up. He did so, and it became a staff once more.

When God calls us to something by faith, the temptation is to wonder what people will think of us if it falls through. People might talk about us or laugh about us or post something on Facebook.

The truth is, they might. But what is also true is those people, and those words, have no power unless I give it to them. It would be so easy to obsess about what is said about our church and me online. To do so is to give power to the naysayers that they haven't earned and that should go elsewhere.

My sister used to say that what terrified the family about me is that I don't care what anyone else thinks. If you are to step into your calling, it's time to put aside your fears of others' perceptions.

Dr. Sam Chand, a fantastic teacher and man of God's Word, gave me an equation. He said growth equals change, change equals loss, and loss equals pain. In other words, if something is growing, it's changing. Nothing can grow without changing, right?

In 1 Corinthians 13:11, Paul said it like this: "When I was a child, I spoke like a child. When I became a man, I put away childish things." In other words, my growth required change, and my change required loss. There were some things that I couldn't carry around with me anymore. I had to let them go. Some things in life are very hard to let go of.

You have friendships in your life right now that aren't going with you to the next level no matter how badly you want them to. They are not a part of your destiny. They were a part of a season, not a destiny. You need to learn who is brick and mortar and who is scaffolding. Some people will help you build to the next level. Then, there are some people that God has destined to be in your life for the rest of your life. It would help if you started making some determination between those who are scaffolding and those who are brick and mortar. You have to be willing to endure the pain of letting some people and some things go.

Some people will never successfully make a transition. You probably know people who are precisely the same as they were 40 years ago. For these people, the fear of change still outweighs the pain they are experiencing. They're not ready to let go of that relationship holding them back or inflicting harm upon them. They're not prepared to walk away from that person who diminishes their dreams and interferes with their purpose.

However, if you are to transform and change and grow, you have to dare to cut off these damaging relationships. You will have to let go of some things. It might hurt, but staying put will be infinitely more damaging and stifling.

BUT LORD...

Moses had had quite a row with the Lord at this point. Upon hearing his commission, he had asked who he is, who God is to send him, and what to do if things fall apart, and he was not done yet! In one last attempt to sidestep his call, he reminded God of his inadequate speaking ability.

Have you ever asked someone to help you move over the weekend, and you get a barrage of questions? *How many rooms? How heavy is the furniture? What kind of truck do you have? Who else will be there? What time do we need to be there?* After a while, it becomes pretty clear that said friend doesn't want to help you move.

Moses asked question after question and finally resorted to a flat-out excuse. He reminded the Lord that he was not a great speaker. Never has been, probably never will be. The Lord has the wrong guy.

The Lord didn't mince words in His response: "Who has made man's mouth? ... Is it not I, the Lord?" (Exodus 4:11, ESV)

You've probably heard it said that if you want to make the Lord laugh, tell Him your plans. I think if you're going to make Him angry, tell Him your limitations. What Moses didn't understand—what most of us don't understand—is that God doesn't ask things of us because of our strengths. He does so because of our weaknesses. It is through those that His power is perfected.

God asks you to do something no human can do, so you don't get any credit for it. He wants to do something so unique that nobody will ever make the mistake of thinking you did it.

There is a story about a mouse that was getting ready to go across a bridge when an elephant approached. The mouse climbed up on the back of the elephant, and the elephant started to cross that bridge, swinging and shaking the bridge the whole way as it creaked under the weight of the elephant. When they finally made it to the other side, that mouse jumped off and looked at the elephant and said, "We really shook that bridge, didn't we?"

At the end of your life, you're going to look at God and say, "We did some stuff!"

God will say, "We sure did. You climbed on my back and let me show my strength through your life. You let me do things beyond what you could ask. You relied on my strength—not yours, my ability—not your ability, my gifts—not your gifts. And because of that, we shook this together."

It's up to you to decide if you are ready for the transition God is placing before you. If so, the thing that could change your life is not in your future. It's in your hand; it's within reach. One of Moses' most distinguishing characteristics was his staff. It was his brand.

Interestingly, he and the staff didn't team up until his first transition had occurred. He didn't grow up in Egypt with a staff in hand.

That became a part of his life when he was banished to the desert and became a shepherd.

When Moses encountered the burning bush and started throwing out his questions and excuses, God wasted no time in incorporating the staff. When Moses said, "What if they don't believe me?" God told him to throw down his staff.

This is incredibly counterintuitive! As a shepherd, that staff was a lifeline. It's what he used to keep the herd together and to defend them and himself from predators. As God prepared Moses to step into this calling, He told him to rid himself of the thing that represented control and order.

When you encounter transition moments in life, one of the first things you have to relinquish is control. Moses had been a ruler in Egypt. He'd been in control of a lot of things. He'd wielded a lot of power. Now, he was ruling over sheep. His congregants had changed significantly, but he was still in control. Now, a God he had just met asked him to throw down the one thing that represented control.

I'm not a golfer. It's just not my pace or my idea of fun. However, I do know a thing or two about golf. For those who are just picking up the game, a telltale sign of a novice is one who tightens his or her grip on the club. It makes the swing inaccurate and reduces the distance the ball will ultimately travel. You have to loosen your grip to improve your shot.

It's pretty remarkable to consider the impact that our body language, particularly the ways in which we use our hands, has upon how we are perceived. A behavioral scientist once said to observe the way you shake hands. Typically, by the end of the handshake, one hand will be on top, indicating the dominant individual in the handshake exchange. This has pretty ancient origins. In Roman times, they did not shake hands standing up; they were sitting down, and it was like an arm-wrestling match to see whose hand would get on top. Thus, we have the saying "the upper hand."

The way you hold your hands is indicative of the control you have or are trying to convey when you speak. When Moses showed up to this conversation at the bush, he was in complete control. But God said, if you are to ever go from being a shepherd on the far side of the desert to being a deliverer, you have to relinquish your control and receive what I have for you.

Moses had the staff in his hands. God told Moses to throw it down.

What is God telling you to throw down today? Is there something in your life that you think you control? Your marriage? Your kids? Your finances? Your future? God says if you want it to be blessed, let go of it. You don't control whatever it is you're holding onto; it controls you. You are being controlled by it because you're hanging on to something that you were never meant to be in charge of, and until you let it go and receive what God has for you, that thing will continue to control you. You have to throw it down. Until you do, it will only be a staff. But the moment you throw it down, it becomes a tool for miracles,

God is in the habit of taking the most common thing in your life and doing the most miraculous thing through it because that's when He gets the glory. David said, "I'm going to fight Goliath." He was offered armor and a sword and decided, "That's okay. I've got this sling."

Samson slayed a thousand Philistines. He didn't use grenades or swords or rockets. He used the jawbone of a donkey. God says the person who will see the miracle in the common is the person for whom He is going to provide. Why? Because that requires faith.

Here's the big idea: You have more than you think you do. You can do more than you think you can do. It's all in your hand.

So Moses threw down the staff. He let go of control, and it became a snake, and he ran. He assumed God would create something miraculous. Instead, God created the thing he feared. Why? Because faith will always command you to confront what you're afraid of.

Everything Moses knew was turned upside down. He knows these kinds of snakes are dangerous. You don't touch them—especially by the tail. But that's precisely what God asked him to do. Moses started to run, but God commanded him to pick up the snake. He commanded him to confront his fear. He knew that if Moses ran then, he would run when it mattered. He knew if Moses did not entirely surrender to and trust Him them, there was no way he would be able to do so in front of Pharaoh. If Moses couldn't confront his fears and trust issues alone in the desert with a snake, what would he do at the Red Sea?

This is the moment when those first two questions come back into play. *Who am I? Who are you?*

In these moments, you have to say, "I know I am not, but I know I AM." I don't have what it takes to save this marriage. I know I am not, but thank God, I know I AM. I know I don't have what it takes to turn my finances around. I know I am not, but I know I AM. Speak that over your life. *I know I am not, but I know I AM.* When the great I AM says you will, you will. He is speaking a new prophecy over your life.

His staff hallmarked Moses' transitions. We don't know where it came from or who gave it to him. It doesn't matter. The rod was not the source of his power. With it, he turned the Nile to blood and parted the Red Sea, but it wasn't the staff that contained or gave any power. It was God who empowered the staff. You must always be aware that your gift is not where you place your faith or draw your strength. Unless God blesses you or blesses your gift, you can't do anything.

Maybe one of the starkest lessons to learn from Moses came toward the end of his life. The people of Israel were wandering in the desert, and they were thirsty. God told Moses to speak to a stone, and water would pour forth. Moses was out of sorts that day. He had total faith in his staff, allowed his emotions to get the better of him, and hit the stone with his stick. The water flowed, and everyone's thirst was quenched, but that act of defiance denied Moses entry into the Promised Land. God told him he would see it, but he would never reach it.

Wouldn't it be awful to spend your whole life being used by God only to get to the end and miss out on your entire purpose because you began to worship your gift more than you worship God?

When our son, Rush, was nearly ten months old, we had a mobile of moons and stars hanging in his room that he was fascinated with. One day, while Kim was holding him, he was reaching up toward it, trying to get his tiny hands on those mesmerizing, floating objects. Kim had to tell him, "I'm sorry, but Mommy can't lift you up there right now."

I reached over and said, "Give him to me."

I took him and held him over my head, so he could finally touch those moons and stars that had been out of reach until Daddy showed up.

Don't ever let others convince you that something is out of reach. Your life has a purpose, and it will involve and require seasons of transition and change. It won't always be easy, but your Heavenly Father is always there to hold you through the challenges. Commit today to be open to the change. Believe that God has already equipped you with everything you need to accomplish the purpose for which He created you. And when you reach out in faith, commit to reaching out again and again until you have achieved your purpose. If you can believe, the dream is within reach.

The Big Idea

No experience is wasted. That which can change your
life isn't in the future; it's within your hands.
What experience have you been allowing to hold you back? What
is it that you feel you need in order to live into your purpose?

Prayer

*Father, thank You for calling me to more. Thank You for using
every part of my story to fulfill the purpose for which You have
created me. Give me the courage, the creativity, and the humility
to accept my call, lean on You, and give You control of my future.*

chapter 7

TUNED BY TENSION

Breaking the Limit of Conflict

*And we know that **for** those who love God all **things** work together*
*for **good**, **for** those who are called according to his purpose.*
—Romans 8:28 (ESV)

Life is a series of pulls back and forth … A tension of opposites, like
a pull on a rubber band. Most of us live somewhere in the middle. A
wrestling match … Which side wins? Love wins. Love always wins.
—Mitch Albom [16]

I could feel my breath catch in my throat as my lungs struggled to reconcile the news my brain had just received. For a moment, it seemed as though disbelief would permanently occupy the space that had held oxygen just seconds ago.

It was 4 AM when my mom called with the news. My sister had passed out and was headed to the hospital. Without giving my head

---

16 Mitch Albom. (n.d.). AZQuotes.com. Retrieved January 06, 2021, from AZQuotes.com Web site: https://www.azquotes.com/quote/343877.

or heart time to process this news, I forced air into my lungs, got in the car, and sped to the hospital.

After dropping the rest of the family at the entrance, I frantically scoured the parking lot for a space. By the time I found one and made it upstairs, I turned the corner and heard the sound I dreaded—the sound of crying delivered the news before anyone even said a word.

She was gone. Elena was just 40. And she was gone. Her life had been so vibrant. A compelling speaker, she had been an incredibly influential leader in the church. Men and women of all ages had been impacted by her life and ministry, all would feel the stinging pain of her early departure. But without question, that pain would be felt most acutely by her husband, Nick, and their two children. Hollie, her 17-year-old daughter, and Luke, her 13-year-old son, would have to relearn how to live in a world their mother was no longer a part of. The sudden, traumatic nature of her passing would only make it harder. Her kids and husband didn't have time to prepare for this. The shock of her death would stay with them for years to come.

While they were grieving a mother and a wife, I was blindsided by the loss of my sister. It felt like the bottom of my world dropped out from under me. I could hardly breathe as I tried to wrap my head around this impossibility.

Surely, there had been a mistake. Surely, God wouldn't take her home so soon without even giving me a chance to say good-bye.

The pain was searing. I couldn't quite reconcile such an unspeakable loss and a good, loving God. As the battle of acceptance raged inside my mind, Romans 8:28 played on a loop in between my thoughts of shock and disbelief.

"And we know that for those who love God all things work together for good, for those who are called according to his purpose" (Romans 8:28, ESV).

In the moment, I struggled to even want to find any good in losing my sister so suddenly and tragically. How could there possibly be anything about this that was good? Over time, I've come to realize that I was looking for good in the wrong places. It wasn't good that she died. It wasn't good that she was gone. Death and absence are not good. However, God was with our family as we stood shoulder to shoulder with a pain like we had never known—and God is good.

There's additional subtext within this verse that is crucial for understanding the meaning of this passage. When Paul states that all things will eventually turn out well for those who love the Lord, he acknowledges that things aren't necessarily good yet. There is a dichotomy between the present struggle and future hope. Two opposing forces are at work here—one that is pulling us toward heaven and one that anchors us to the earth. It's a tug-of-war that began in the Garden of Eden.

When God created the heavens and the earth and the animals and every other part of this magnificent universe, He declared it all to be "good." When He created man and woman, they were "very good." If everything in creation, everything under the sun, is intrinsically good, why do we have earthquakes and cancer? We have marriage, which is good, but we also have divorce. There is life, but death is inevitable.

How did the bad enter the picture if all of God's creation was so good? The answer comes down to choice. Adam and Eve chose Satan over God, ushering pain, hardship, and suffering into the world God created out of love. From that point on, people have had to contend with affliction. For centuries, we have inherited and harbor an ache that won't ever entirely subside this side of heaven.

Yet, Scripture says that God longs for us to live life to the full, to know joy here and now. In the middle of loss, grief, and illness, however, it's easy to forget God's deepest desire is to love us and receive our love in return. Instead, when bad things happen, we often conclude that God can't be good. A good God wouldn't allow such suffering.

That's a short-sighted perspective. The reality is that, while we endure hardship, we remain tethered to God's unconditional love. It's much easier to see and feel that love at certain times in life than in seasons of pain. Regardless of our capacity or willingness to accept His love, it never moves or changes.

If you've ever tuned a guitar or observed someone else tuning one, you probably know that there are usually six strings that run along the neck, or fretboard, of the guitar. Those strings are secured at the bridge at the bottom of the instrument, then run lengthwise to the top, where they are wound around tuning pegs.

You change the pitch of each string by loosening or tightening the string on those pegs. The tighter the string is wound, the higher the pitch; that pitch then lowers as the string is loosened. The goal is to tune each string to the exact pitch for which it was designed to sound good when played with the other strings. The tuner accomplishes this by adjusting the tension on each string.

In many ways, you and I are like that guitar. On one end, we are anchored by God's unchanging love. At the other, our losses and victories, joys and sorrows, health or sickness are turning the tuning pegs, loosening and tightening, raising and lowering the pitch, improving or damaging our overall sound.

Like the guitar, if we are to function at all, tension is required. Physiologically, it's tension within our bodies that flexes and releases our muscles, allowing us to move our bones. Emotionally and spiritually, tension enables us to create and maintain relationships, experience joy, and live lives fueled by intention rather than apathy. For better or worse, the tension in our lives and how we respond to it will shape the quality of life that we experience and our capacity to fulfill our God-given purpose.

TENSION VS. STRESS

A quick Google search of "reducing tension in life" pulls up over 120 million results. Interestingly, not one of the first-page headlines includes the word "tension." Instead, they focus on stress—managing, reducing, and eliminating it, which makes sense given the statistics.

According to the American Institute of Stress, 83% of U. S. workers suffer from work-related stress, which causes 120,000 deaths and $190 billion in healthcare costs every year.[17]

Tension and stress are not the same thing. Tension is a necessary, inevitable, and permanent fixture of the human experience. Stress occurs when the appropriate amount of tension is exceeded. Think

17 42 Worrying Workplace Statistics. *The American Institute of Stress.* Retrieved on December 27, 2020. Website: https://www.stress.org/42-worrying-workplace-stress-statistics.

of the guitar. It's entirely possible to keep turning that tuning peg tighter and tighter until the string pops. Too much tension resulted in a degree of stress the string wasn't designed to withstand and, therefore, it didn't. It couldn't.

I doubt there are many people who would deny that stress is harmful. We all know that work and commitment overload usually lead to burnout or worse. Yet, while we often complain that we don't have time to accomplish everything and are then perpetually stressed, we also seem to wear our busyness like a badge of honor.

Over the past decade or so, social media has elevated stress and activity bragging to an Olympic-level sport, primarily fueled by FOMO: the fear of missing out. Did you know that you touch your phone an average of 1,617 times a day? There are only 1,440 minutes in a 24-hour period, meaning you are touching your phone more than there are minutes in the day, not to mention you are asleep for at least a few of those hours.

Don't dismiss this as a frivolous conversation that doesn't apply to you and your current struggles. Our continued and growing addiction to our phones and social media is causing quantifiable problems with genuine repercussions. Imagine you're at work, and you get the itch to hop on Facebook to check out that coworker who may not have showed up to work that day. You check it for two minutes. Thirty minutes later, you do the same and continue the pattern throughout the day.

Two minutes might seem trivial, but once you get on social media, it takes, on average, 23 minutes and 15 seconds to fully reengage with your original project or assignment. If this is a perpetual pattern, guess how much you will accomplish during the workday? You're so distracted that you can't get anything done. Productivity is sidelined, your personal advancement stalls, and in five years, you'll be looking around wondering what you've done with all your time.

You do it at home, too. You may be throwing a party but then hear about another party and jump on Facebook to compare the guest lists, decorations, food, and so on. Maybe you are at your child's basketball game and miss his or her layup because your head was buried in your phone.

CREATURES OF HABIT

Chances are, you are fully aware of your habits and aren't particularly proud of them, yet you can't find the steel inside of you necessary to relinquish them. When I think of the habits that I want to break but can't or don't, I often think about what Paul wrote in Romans 7: "For I have the desire to do what is right, but not the ability to carry it out. For I do not do the good I want, but the evil I do not want is what I keep on doing. Now if I do what I do not want, it is no longer I who do it, but sin that dwells within me" (vv. 18-20, ESV).

Paul describes the tension that resides within all of us that dictates what we do and don't do. I find great comfort in knowing that even a warrior of faith like Paul struggled with inner conflict. It's oddly reassuring to see how powerfully God used a flawed man, just like the rest of us.

There's another piece of information to pull from this, though, that's more than a little unsettling. When Paul asserts that even he struggles with willpower, it's an affirmation that this is a real battle within all of us. Over the years, brilliant scientists, engineers, and innovators have observed this same phenomenon and developed ways to exploit it. Oddly enough, those sophisticated algorithms and techniques that get us to keep coming back to Facebook, Twitter, and the like began with a Harvard professor and some pigeons in the early 70s.

B. F. Skinner was a psychology professor who noticed many similarities between the brain functions of pigeons and humans. He conducted an experiment in which he placed pigeons within a confined area. When hit by a pigeon, a button would turn a light on and give the pigeon a treat. Then, another pigeon would come along, do the same thing, and the cycle would repeat.

Skinner set up this button, and whenever the pigeon hit the button, a light would come on, and a treat would come out. The pigeon would walk up, hit the button, a light would come on, and a treat would come out. It would then eat the treat. Another pigeon would come up and do the same thing. After several days, Skinner altered the process, so the treats would fall at random intervals. The buttons still got pushed, and the lights still came on, but there might not be a treat. While initially, he thought the pigeons would hit the button less frequently, the pigeons hit the button twice as often when the treat was unpredictable.

Years later, Facebook created a similar button for all of us humans. We know it as the "Like" button. Like Skinner, Facebook will disseminate your Likes at random intervals. You may have two Likes on your latest post, then five minutes later, ten Likes. Just like the pigeons, you'll keep checking back with increasing frequency to see how many

Likes you've accumulated. The model has been so successful, Twitter, Instagram, and YouTube have also adopted it.

With "Likes" now the reigning social currency, many people have adapted their entire lives to generate more and more. Rather than enhance the quality of our lives or make us feel better about ourselves, the obsession with social media and social relevancy has made us, overall, less happy and healthy.

As wellness coach Elizabeth Scott reported: "Unsurprisingly, adolescents use social networking sites at a high rate and may experience FOMO as a result. Interestingly, however, FOMO acts as a mechanism that triggers higher social networking usage. Girls experiencing depression tend to use social networking sites at a greater rate, while, for boys, anxiety was a trigger for greater social media use. This shows that increased use of social media can lead to higher stress rates caused by FOMO."[18]

REST IN THE MIDDLE

When FOMO dictates your life, you've surrendered your time, your potential, and possibly your mental wellbeing. As your time and focus are increasingly occupied by competition and comparison, your sense of inadequacy is likely to follow suit. Without even realizing it, you are generating so much tension in your life, your capacity to withstand the tug-of-war between good and bad is compromised.

---

18 Scott, E. "How to Deal with FOMO in Your Life." *Verywellmind*, February 19, 2020. Website: https://www.verywellmind.com/how-to-cope-with-fomo-4174664#:~:text=FOMO%2C%20or%20 %22fear%20of%20missing,people%20are%20 at%20greater%20risk.

When an unexpected tragedy or blow hits, just like a string that is wound too tightly, you can break.

There has been nothing more unexpected in my life than losing my sister. Elena was young and healthy. She simply went to bed one night and never woke up. While my grief over losing her seemed to swallow me whole, the coinciding anxiety that crept into my life seemed like it would break me. I began to self-medicate, trying to drag myself from one day to the next. Just like an instrument can fall out of tune, my life was all over the place. Extreme lows followed extreme highs. There was discord from day to day in my life.

On the one hand, I was pastoring a church; on the other, I was on the verge of a breakdown. The longer I tried to fix myself, the weaker I became. I was turning that tuning peg tighter and tighter, exceeding the amount of tension I was created to handle, to the point I was going to snap.

Finally, one Saturday night, I clearly remember standing in front of a mirror and saying, "God, I can't do this anymore."

The next day, my wife prodded me down the aisle during our church service. Every step seemed heavier and more grueling than before until I made it to the front and simply crumbled. People began to surround me and pray for me as I continued to acknowledge to God that I couldn't handle this on my own. God answered, "You don't have to. You have been crucified with Christ, and it is He who lives within you."

As I let His words wash over me, it was as though the tension let up. For the first time in a very long time, I felt free from anxiety, fear, and the torture of worry. What's more, I now had a renewed understanding of what Paul meant when he said God works all things for good. More than ever before, I realized God would use even my deepest pain to reveal His glory.

That doesn't mean God eliminated my pain. Instead, He helped me release it into His hands. Up to this point, I had been generating stress by trying to make something good come from something so tragic. God reminded me that not only is that not my responsibility; it's not even within my capabilities. What's more, I could see that God wasn't using the struggle and pain to torment me but rather to tune me.

I don't know how He did it then and continues to do it now, but faith tells me I don't have to know. Faith tells me simply to rest within the tension as if it were a hammock. One day at a time, I continue to learn to relax in the middle of the tension, knowing that, even though I don't understand it, somehow God's going to take what's bad and make it work for my good.

In all likelihood, I will never understand why God took my sister home while I'm on this side of heaven. What I do know is that His ways are higher and wiser than mine, and while I try to reconcile this loss within the context of my life, God is at work within the context of eternity.

The Big Idea

God designed us to live within the tension of heaven and earth, using our challenges to tune and refine us. What loss or grievance are you trying to reconcile today? Are you willing to release the grip you have over your tragedy and allow God to transform your pain?

Prayer

Father, thank You for working beyond my understanding. Please give me the faith to trust You with my broken pieces. Help me remember that no matter what comes my way, You will never let me go. Help me rest within the tension between life and its many struggles and Your unwavering, redeeming love.

chapter 8

A ROOM WITH A VIEW
Breaking the Limit of Sight

*Whatever is true, whatever is honorable, whatever is
just, whatever is pure, whatever is lovely, whatever
is commendable, if there is any excellence, if there is
anything worthy of praise, think about these things.*
—Philippians 4:8 (ESV)

*The sweetest thing in all my life has been the longing—to reach
the Mountain, to find the place where all the beauty came from.*
—C. S. Lewis[19]

Once, two men were very sick and placed in the same hospital room. One bed was next to the window, while the other was on the opposite side of the room. Only the man next to the window could see out of it. Every day, he would raise his bed to look out and describe what he was seeing to the other man.

---

19 C. S. Lewis. (n.d.). AZQuotes.com. Retrieved December 13, 2020, from AZQuotes.com. Web site: https://www.azquotes.com/quote/349301.

One day, he said, "This is beautiful! There's a park right outside, and kids are playing in the grass. I see a dog chasing a ball. The sun is so bright!"

The next day he said, "Oh, you should see it today. There's a fountain, and it's shooting so high in the air that people are tossing coins and making wishes."

Even though he was weak and tired from his illness, each day, he would raise his bed and paint a picture of what was outside to his roommate. One day, it was beautiful flowers and budding trees. The next, it was gorgeous green grass, birds flitting around, and families enjoying the sunshine.

Every day when he shared the beautiful view, the other man just became more and more bitter, thinking, *Why does he get to see out the window, and I don't?*

As the days passed, he grew so bitter and angry that one night, when the other man wasn't looking, he poisoned his drink, and the man died. Once the orderlies had removed the body, he asked the nurse if he could have the bed next to the window.

"Absolutely," she replied. "It's available."

He was so excited as the aides helped him move from one bed to the other. Finally, he would get to see the park and the children and the beautiful flowers. The view that the first man had would finally be his to enjoy.

As soon as he settled into the bed, he hit the button to raise the bed until he could see above the windowsill, past the blinds, into the great outdoors that had been kept from him. However, the man was shocked to realize that there was nothing but a brick wall beyond the windowpane. There were no trees, no park, no flowers, or children playing. After all his bitterness and his scheming, he saw nothing but bricks.

THE VIEW FROM THE TOP

If you've ever had the chance to travel and stay in a nice hotel, you know that (generally speaking) if you have the choice, you want to stay in the room with the best view. If I go to the ocean, I don't want to stare at a parking lot. I want to see the waves and watch the sun glint on the water; I want to take in the breathtaking view of a sunset at sea.

If I'm staying in a city, I don't want to see the walls of other buildings or hotels. I want to see the rise and fall of the cityscape. What are the defining features that set this place apart? Give me something to look at that I can remember!

While it makes sense that anyone would want to enjoy a good view, have you ever stopped to think about why? What is it about the sensory experience of a beautiful perspective that is so compelling? Well, you don't have to look far to realize that filling our minds with beautiful, lovely things isn't just pleasant; it's biblical.

Philippians 4:8 (ESV) tells us, "Whatever is true, whatever is honorable, whatever is just, whatever is pure, whatever is lovely, whatever is commendable, if there is any excellence, if there is anything worthy of praise, think about these things."

When we're on vacation, when we're staring out of the penthouse, it's pretty easy to take in the beauty. But, when we're at home, it tends to be more challenging. Although we're surrounded by the people we love in a house we've worked hard for, sometimes the comforts of home look less attractive and more cumbersome.

Other times, there may be nothing in sight that's even the least bit attractive. Think of that man in the hospital. Day after day, his view was nothing but a brick wall. There were no scenes of happiness or beauty for him to enjoy or to share. But somehow, that didn't stop him from enjoying the view. Not only did he choose not to let his drab surroundings bring him down, he decided to open his mind, imagine the beauty he knew existed in the world, and then share it with someone else.

So how is it that different people can look at the same thing yet see wildly different scenes? Once, Kim and I were visiting Los Angeles and staying on one of the top floors. The window went out a little bit over the edge of the room, so you could climb up into it and look down. I wanted to see what things looked like, so the first thing I did was head for the window.

It was spectacular. I felt like I could see for miles around. I took in the city, watching the busyness of LA life down below, absolutely thrilled that this would be our view for our entire stay. As I took it in, I called, "Kim, you've got to see this!"

"No, I can see enough from right here," she answered. I heard a slight tremble in her voice, and as I turned around, I could see that she was literally hugging the wall. Her face was white, her head was shaking, and it was clear that she would not be fully participating in the 75th-floor experience.

Why? Her fear was getting in the way. It was holding her back from leaning into that moment. As I think about my perspectives and points of view, I understand that the one thing that can more quickly destroy my view, block me from seeing beauty and possibility ahead, is myself. Plus, if I'm not careful, things can come into my life and take away my view—or worse, take away my dream or my vision.

That's what the enemy wants to do. Amid everything going on in your life, he is out to take your view because if he can get your view, he can get your vision. If he can get your vision, he can get your dream. If he can get your dream, he's got your family. And do you know who he'll use to take your view away faster than anybody else? You! Me! No one can take away my view more quickly than I can. However, time and again, despite all that I do to distort my view, God has always been right there to restore it.

I will never forget one of the most challenging seasons of our lives. As I took the stage to preach that week, my heart was crumbling. We had never been that close to quitting the ministry. Kim's words played and replayed in my head: "I'm done. I'm out of here. This isn't worth it."

No one else knew what was going on in our lives. I would get up and preach that God wants to heal and bless you and make you whole, while on the inside, my life had just fallen apart. I'll never forget around this time a dream that I had one night that I believe came from God.

I was in a huge hotel, with a long staircase running to the front door. Suddenly our daughter, Saige, dashed outside toward a small, ramshackle house with a tiny porch and a single window with jagged glass dotting the frame. Naturally, I ran after her and watched in horror as she crawled through that window into a room full of decaying rusty nails, hammers, and all sorts of dangerous objects that are a parent's worst nightmare.

I raced to the window, reached in, and grabbed Saige, shouting, "What are you doing? You could have been killed! Don't you ever come back to a place like this! Come on. We're going." No sooner had we reached the door of the hotel than I saw her crawling back through the window of that house of horrors. Emotions churning, I ran back and said, "What are you doing? Why would you go back?"

Gathering her into my arms, I walked back to the hotel. As I reached the long staircase, a hand grabbed me from behind, picked me up, turned me around, and held me. Across from the stairs, I saw an image so powerful I later drew it in my journal. It was a profile of a king draped in purple, with a large crown on his head. Just beyond His finger, I saw the words of 2 Corinthians 4:7: "We have this treasure in earthen vessels, that the excellence of the power may be of God and not of us" (NKJV). The voice belonging to the hand that held me from behind said, "He's got this."

When I start to lose my view, when things get distorted, and I can no longer visualize what's ahead of me, I have to remember that the solution will not be about what I can do or how good I am. I am nothing but an earthen vessel. What's valuable is the treasure on the inside—God's power, not mine.

So, when you look at what's ahead of you and take in your view, it's essential to stop thinking about what's now and start focusing on what's next. It's easy to confuse what faith is all about. The opposite of faith isn't fear; the opposite of faith is certainty. You may be quite sure of what you see before you right now. But no matter how discouraging or blurry your perspective may be in this moment, God is holding you, and He holds a beautiful future He can't wait for you to see. You just need to get out of the way first.

LESS REACTIVE, MORE INTROSPECTIVE

Over the years, I have learned that I don't do a very good job hiding what I'm feeling. No one ever has to wonder what Pastor Eric is feeling. Turns out, having your gut reaction written all over your face isn't always a good look. Even more damaging than the look across your face, potentially, is what comes out of it.

Have you ever had to run damage control after letting things fly? You're making the rounds to other offices or cubicles within earshot, praying your boss hasn't caught wind of your verbal free fall. Or, more likely, you may be living through or cleaning up the aftermath of your latest online exposition.

Whether it's Facebook, Twitter, a blog, or a comments section, social media has made it deceptively easy for everyone to let everyone else know exactly how they're feeling about everything at any given time. It is convenient to air your thoughts, judgments, reactions, and criticisms behind a veil of false anonymity. For some reason, when we hide behind a screen, we assume we're untraceable and invincible. Maybe even worse, when we type words that we would never dream of saying to a person's face, we don't even care if people know who said it.

There's such a disconnect between how we live in the real world and how we interact online. We've convinced ourselves that it doesn't matter, it doesn't affect other people, and undoubtedly, that it doesn't impact our visions, dreams, or plans. Seemingly, we're just speaking, typing, or reacting from the heart.

Jeremiah 17:9 (ESV) says, "The heart is deceitful above all things, and desperately sick; who can understand it?" It's not a rousing endorsement, but it's a perfect tool. The enemy will use your heart to defeat your destiny—not because you are a bad or a wicked person. But the things you feel, say, or share in a moment of reaction will inevitably result in consequences you won't be able to undo.

Chances are, you may realize your post wasn't in the best taste. Maybe you delete that comment, but do you follow up with an admission of wrong? Or an apology? As much as we want to take back that moment and its repercussions, oftentimes, we can't. We're like toothpaste. Whatever comes out of the tube isn't going back in.

That means we need to veer away from reaction towards introspection. Of course, there are times when people have their opinions about me, choose to share them openly, and I want to fire back. These are the moments when Kim is my wisdom. More than once, I've said, "Kim, how does this sound?"

She'll say, "Delete that. You're bigger than that."

You need people of wisdom like that in your life, who will tell you that you don't need to write that or say that.

Proverbs 4:5-7 (ESV) says, "Get wisdom; get insight; do not forget, and do not turn away from the words of my mouth. Do not forsake her, and she will keep you; love her, and she will guard you. The beginning of wisdom is this: Get wisdom, and whatever you get, get insight." Wisdom says you may have the freedom to say something, but should you? There may be times you are tempted, but wisdom will tell you to rise above it. When you do, you are closer to attaining your vision, your goals, your room with a view.

CHOP THE RIGHT TREE

Outside our house, we had two trees. The one in front was huge. It completely blocked the house. You could hardly see it from the outside, and from the inside, it was nearly impossible to see past it. It was huge, and it had those little seeds that would drop by the thousands. They stuck to everything and were constantly getting tracked through the garage and throughout the house. The tree had become a nuisance and had to go.

Then there is another tree in the back of the house. It sits right up on our deck, entirely blocks the sun's heat during the first half of the day, framing the sunset just beautifully as the day comes to an end. It's a good tree, a great tree. But it had been sick and started dropping its leaves.

So, I called some people to help me with my trees. The one in front had to go, the one in the back needed some help, but it had to stay! That would not be an easy mistake to remedy. That's why contractors will mark trees with ribbon or spray paint to indicate if the tree should stay or go. First of all, removing a tree is hard work and takes planning and time. And if you chop down the wrong one, not only have you wasted your time and energy, but it will take years for that tree to grow back.

Every day, you have a finite amount of energy and time. You need to show deference when you decide what you're going to focus on and reserve your highest energy levels—your most creative output—for those things that are not only gratifying but move you closer to your purpose. When I am full of energy, and my mind is sharp, I am more empathetic, more creative, and I am kinder to people. I want to reserve the best of me for those things and those people that matter.

We went to a root beer stand once, and Saige got this giant root beer float. I had a nice car, a clean car, and Saige was in the backseat when I heard the "Uh-oh." That only means one thing—a mess. Probably a big, sticky mess that will leave at least a hint of a stain. Kim thought I was going to get upset. Part of me wanted to, but another part began to tell myself that I probably wouldn't even have this car five years from now. Was it worth it to ruin this moment by throwing a fit?

Losing your temper takes energy. It drains your fuel, and it gets you nowhere other than farther from those you love, with a depleted supply of all that you need to finish out the day. Your mind and your time are too valuable. Don't waste them, and don't lose your focus chopping down the wrong tree.

CLOSE THE SITUATION ROOM

If you ever watch CNN, you know that it has a show called *The Situation Room*. Why? Because every day, without fail, they discover a situation upon which to report. It's one thing for a news network to search out its situations, but do you also have a situation room? Are you always on the hunt for something that will inevitably make you upset? Or alarmed? Or angry? Or sad?

The truth is, we don't need to encounter a situation every day. It's human nature to look for everything around you that's wrong, and it's easy to find! One week after a service, some people complimented the way I looked. They said I looked dapper. It made me feel good! Then one person said, "What I loved the best about your outfit was the way you rocked those white socks."

I looked at that person and said, "I wasn't wearing any socks. My ankles are just that white."

If people want to find something wrong with me, they won't have to look very far. Anybody can find something wrong with somebody or some situation. You can also choose to be the person to find the good in others, the beauty in the world around you. You can be the person to find the hope inside of a situation—hope that turns a crisis into an opportunity.

When those two men in the hospital stared at a brick wall, they saw vastly different views. The first man chose to see beauty, happiness, hope, and a world that he still wanted to be a part of, so much so that he shared his incredible view with another man who desperately needed a sunny day.

The second man went the easier route. He chose to be bitter—bitter of what he thought he was being denied in his bed far across the room, and bitter when he realized the truth that lay on the other side of that window.

It's easy to choose bitterness. It takes a lot more energy, wisdom, perspective, and intention to choose to be better. That's the life God wants for you and me, though. He wants us to see sunshine and cloudless skies. He wants us to see the possibilities. He wants us to see them, read them, think about them, and fill our minds and hearts and perspectives with lovely, good, and holy things.

As you focus on what's next, make sure you're burning your fuel in the right places. Make sure you're chopping down the right trees. Don't spend your time looking for problems or dwelling on past failures. Lift your eyes to heaven. Allow the Holy Spirit to fill your mind, elevate your actions and your decisions, and take in the beauty of the view from the top.

The Big Idea

Bitterness blocks; forgiveness flows. If you choose to be bitter, you will block every blessing of God from coming into your life. Choose to get better; refuse to get bitter. What grudge are you holding onto that is blocking your view? Are you spending your energy and time on things that will release blessings or harbor bitterness?

Prayer

Father, no matter what I go through today, no matter what I face, I trust that You've got this. Help me have the confidence and the humility to let You hold my life.

chapter 9

A BLESSING CALLED REJECTION

Breaking the Limit of Exclusion

*"The stone that the builders rejected has become the **cornerstone**;*
this was the Lord's doing, and it is marvelous in our eyes ..."
Matthew 21:42 (NIV)

One of the greatest forms of direction for your life is rejection.
—Dag Heward Mills[20]

In 1919, a young man was fired from his job at the *Kansas City Star* by an editor who said he "lacked imagination and had no good ideas."[21] By the 1930s, this same man's company was $4 million in debt.

In 1937, he released the first full-length animated feature film called *Snow White and the Seven Dwarfs*. The film's overwhelming success not only cleared his debt, it paved the way for the construction

---

20 Mills, D. H. Retrieved on December 30, 2020, from All Christian Quotes. Website: https://www.allchristianquotes.org/quotes/Dag_Heward_Mills/474/.

21 Hodin, R. "35 Famous People Who Were Painfully Rejected Before Making It Big." *Thought Catalog.* Retrieved on December 30, 2020. Website: https://thoughtcatalog.com/rachel-hodin/2013/10/35-famous-people-who-were-painfully-rejected-before-making-it-big/.

of a new Walt Disney Studios in Burbank, California. Walt, the kid who was dismissed for lack of imagination, was on his way.

Everyone loves an underdog story, and Walt's is hard to beat. Perhaps the reason his journey and others like it are so compelling is that we can all identify with rejection. All of us, at some point, in some way, have been shut down, overlooked, or dismissed. Be it a parent, another family member, peer, or colleague, rejection can come from any direction. Maybe you were the kid who never got invited to the parties, or you were picked last in PE class. Perhaps you were let go from or weren't accepted by a company, school, or organization. That rejection letter is from an HR department, but you are well aware that a person is on the other end of that decision.

When it comes to rejection, there are a lot of things I can identify with and understand. However, there are many forms of rejection I haven't lived through and can't fully understand. I'm so thankful that I've never had to wonder if my parents loved or wanted me. I've never known the sting of rejection when a spouse walks away. I don't understand those feelings—but Jesus does. He's acquainted with every rejection you've ever felt. He's acquainted with every grief you've ever felt. We do not have a high priest who has not been touched with the feeling of our infirmities. In other words, He knows how you feel. He knows what you feel.

In Isaiah 53:3 (ESV), there is a prophecy about the Messiah who was yet to come. It said, "He was despised and rejected by men, a **man of sorrow**s and acquainted with grief; and as one from whom men hide their faces he was despised, and we esteemed him not."

Have you ever been somewhere and spotted someone you knew who purposefully avoided eye contact and acted as if he or she had never met you? Have you ever done that to someone else?

That's what happened to Jesus. From his own family to His most faithful disciples, people acted as if they didn't know Him throughout His life. From the cradle to the grave, He experienced what it is not to be wanted.

When Mary first told Joseph she was pregnant with the Son of God, Joseph didn't want anything to do with either of them. Because he was a decent man, he would arrange for Mary to be sent away to raise her child, instead of letting their village stone her for alleged, seemingly apparent indiscretions. But he didn't want to be a part of their lives, nor they a part of his.

On the night of His birth, Mary and Joseph were turned away from inn after inn, leaving them no choice but to deliver their baby in a barn. Throughout His life, He was rejected by His family members, many of whom didn't believe that He was, in fact, the Son of God. His hometown was hostile to Him. The book of Luke records an incident in which Jesus returns to His community, only to be driven out and up to a cliff where they intended to throw Him off.

Jesus faced rejection from people close to him. Knowing everything that was to come, He still humbled Himself. Before He went to the cross, He got on His knees and took off His garments.

I've often wondered if Judas and Peter were sitting next to each other. I wonder whose feet He washed first. Judas was about to betray Him, turning Him over to those who would inflict excruciating torture and pain upon him, yet He willingly washed his feet. Peter was

about to deny Him three times and even curse that he knew Him. Yet Jesus got down and washed their feet, sat with them at a table. He loved them even though they both were about to betray Him.

Jesus was rejected for a host of reasons. He was rejected because He was from the wrong town, from the wrong family, and He got the wrong message. He could preach as long as He continued to heal and give people what they wanted, but the moment He declared He was the Son of God, they were ready to kill Him.

His truth led to rejection. Are you willing to suffer the same? Are you ready to endure rejection for truth? It is doubtful that you're going to make it in this world, standing on the Word of God and not be rejected.

In retrospect, I've come to realize that the rejection I experienced earlier in my life prepared me for the rejection I have experienced because of the pulpit. I survived rocks and BB guns. Social media posts don't phase me. I can preach unequivocal truth. Whatever fault someone may find in my words will not sway me. I will call evil for what it is, and if you reject me for it, I'm cool with that.

REJECTION RATIONALE

To reach a place where you, too, are at peace with being the object of rejection, it's helpful to understand the various forms of rejection. Having some context and insight into the source of rejection you are subject to, or to which you subject others, enables you to reframe a situation and, rather than allow it to consume you, aspire to create something constructive out of what was intended for destruction.

Conditional Rejection

The first type of rejection is conditional rejection. Practically, I accept you as long as you meet my expectations. The moment you fall short, you're out.

This type of behavior reveals a stark lack of grace. People develop these long lists of conditions, calling people to a higher standard than even they can live up to. This is a toxic way to engage with people, is based entirely on performance, and is today's general norm. Everything is performance-based, or so it seems. As damaging as this type of interaction between people can be, there's a real danger of assuming that this type of rejection/acceptance standard also applies to God. It's tempting to assume that God's love for you is also based on performance. And when you fall short, it's natural to conclude that God is done with you.

Nothing could be further from the truth. If I do everything right, God loves me. If I do everything wrong, God still loves me. His grace is something we can't quantify or understand; we must merely receive and accept it.

Emotional Rejection

The second common type of rejection has everything to do with feelings. Emotional rejection takes place when someone is offended or hurt on an emotional level. Some people can never get over their bruised feelings; no matter how many apologies they receive, their wounded emotions hold them back from extending grace, even if the incident was unintentional or a misunderstanding. For those who are ruled by their emotions, the road to forgiveness is long and curvy and may simply be a dead end.

Celebrity Rejection

Rejection type number three is somewhat of a contemporary phenomenon. In an age of social media, influencers, YouTube, and instant access to followers worldwide, a culture of celebrity has taken shape that's, in a word, strange. Popularity and notoriety seem to boil down to the person who can take and post the most pictures, be the most plugged-in, culturally relevant, "woke" individual without offending anyone, and be able to withstand the fluctuations of "cancel culture."

While those of us who do not claim celebrity status might like to stand back and look disapprovingly at the masses of followers hanging on every tweet or post from one influencer or another, it would be too shortsighted to disregard the role all of us play in this culture of celebrity.

When God first knit us together, He gave us a purpose. We were created to worship. Specifically, we were made to worship Him. It doesn't take much, though, for us to shift the focus of our worship from God to the latest trending celebrities. We confuse honor with worship and start worshiping people; we worship the creatures above the Creator. In so doing, we place these people on pedestals of fame, wealth, and talent. They come to represent the dreams we are often too afraid of or unable to pursue. We live vicariously through them and their publicized accomplishments until the latest, greatest, youngest personality steals our attention.

Once their fleeting fame has, well, fled, you're more likely to see them on an infomercial than in a blockbuster. At that point, said celebrities don't get invited to the parties or steal the show on a red carpet. The special treatment is gone, and they are now just trying to get by and pay bills like the rest of us. They are no longer larger than life. Therefore, they can no longer claim celebrity status.

Irrational Rejection

The final rejection type, irrational rejection, is just what it sounds like. It is this type of rejection that makes no sense. There is no logic, yet some people will reject others for no reason at all. No matter how much you talk to them, love them, try to forgive them, they will never accept you. Their rejection is not based on any level of reality. When a parent rejects a child, it's irrational. Regardless of the bridges a child tries to build to reconnect with an estranged parent, the choice to cross that bridge is up to that parent. There is no logical explanation for that kind of behavior.

THE PAIN IS REAL

Not only is it helpful to understand the structure and origin of rejection, but it's also absolutely critical that you acknowledge the genuine damage rejection causes and its long-term implications for our lives.

Not long ago, some scientists did a study on rejection. They took a group of people and put them into a rejection scenario. Throughout the study, the subjects' brains were monitored. When the participants experienced rejection, the same part of the brain that experiences pain lit up.

If you've been physically hurt, like when I broke my finger, you may remember that pain, but it's hard to recall the intensity. If you think back to the last time you were rejected, chances are you can remember each nuance of the pain you experienced. While your brain can't remember physical pain, it never lets go of the emotional pain rejection inflicts.

This is what drives people to self-medicate, turning to drugs or other addictions. They are trying to relieve themselves from the pain, often with devastating consequences. The US Surgeon General issued a warning that young people who are rejected are at a greater risk for adolescent violence than those impacted by drugs, poverty, or gang membership.

There is a condition called RSD, rejection sensitive dysphoria, which is extreme emotional sensitivity and pain triggered by the perception that a person has been rejected or criticized by important people in his or her life. It may also be triggered by a sense of falling short or failing to meet their high standards or other expectations. A person with a spirit of rejection will always be easily offended.

Attempting to combat this condition can be exhausting because it will drive you to do whatever is necessary to avoid rejection. You comment on pictures not because you liked the picture, but you're afraid that someone' will reject you if you don't. You go to weddings or other social gatherings not because you want to, but you fear the rejection that may come your way if you don't. It's a frantic race you can't win because each time you are turned down or sent away, your insecurities are confirmed.

Did you lose the job?

I wasn't qualified anyway.

Did your spouse leave?

I knew I would never be good enough for him (or her).

Get a nasty comment online?

I'm so stupid. Why did I think my opinion mattered in the first place?

Once self-doubt takes hold, it can be next to impossible to get rid of it. The theologian and scholar Henry Nouwen wrote this of self-rejection:

> Over the years, I have come to realize that the greatest trap in our life is not success, popularity, or power, but self-rejection. Success, popularity, and power can indeed present a great temptation, but their seductive quality often comes from the way they are part of the much larger temptation to self-rejection. When we have come to believe in the voices that call us worthless and unlovable, then success, popularity, and power are easily perceived as attractive solutions. The real trap, however, is self-rejection. As soon as someone accuses me or criticizes me, as soon as I am rejected, left alone, or abandoned, I find myself thinking, "Well, that proves once again that I am a nobody." … [My dark side says,] I am no good … I deserve to be pushed aside, forgotten, rejected, and abandoned. Self-rejection is the greatest enemy of the spiritual life because it contradicts the

sacred voice that calls us the "Beloved." Being the Beloved constitutes the core truth of our existence.[22]

Before allowing yourself to sink into that pit of negativity and self-rejection, consider a different perspective. Did you ever think that maybe you were rejected because you exceeded expectations?

This is what happened to Jesus. Every time the Pharisees tried to control Him, He went above them. They thought if He kept exceeding expectations in the minds of the people, they were not going to be able to stop Him. So, their only resort, seemingly, was to kill Him. In other words, his ability to exceed their expectations exposed their failure.

People will get upset when you do better than they do because they could have done better. They just chose not to. When you out-work somebody lazy, that person will attack you because he or she is lazy. Maybe you're being rejected because you're doing better than you think you are.

Rejection is a result of people's vision, not your value. Jesus said it like this: You are so concerned about the speck in their eye, yet you miss the log that's in your eye. The reason you can't see them for what they're worth is that you don't see what's blocking your vision of their value. Some people can't see your worth because there's something they can't see past.

What they'll do is give you their opinion. However, when you know your value, you're not moved by people's views or rejections because there's only one opinion that truly matters—our Heavenly Father's.

What does the Father think about me?
What does God think about me?
What does Jesus think about me?

Jesus' entire life was built upon rejection because it was the only way He could fulfill the purpose for which He had been sent. If the world had not rejected Him, He would never have been sentenced to die. His purpose, however, was to die on the cross.

I'm sure you've asked "Why?" many times throughout your life. I have. Why was I never invited to a football game or to go to prom? It took me a long time to realize that God wasn't allowing me to be rejected to keep me *from* something; instead, He allowed me to be rejected to keep me *for* something.

I can hear the Father say, "You thought you were being rejected, but ultimately you were being separated because I'm going to do something different in your life. There's a reason."

When Jesus was dying on the cross, He cried. "My God, My God, why have you forsaken me?"

However, the familiar translation of that verse doesn't capture the original meaning of the phrase in Jesus' native tongue—Aramaic.

The original meaning of the phrase was, "For this purpose was I kept."

There is a purpose behind your rejection. You may not see it right now, and it can be excruciating, but God has placed you where you are for a purpose.

You know what it's like to be rejected, but is there something in your life that you're rejecting? When someone gets an organ transplant, that person has to start taking anti-rejection drugs. The body doesn't recognize the foreign object and starts attacking that implant meant to save your life. Your body is confused because it thinks that this invader has come in to hurt you, not heal you.

So, your body releases two things: T-cells and antibodies. Is there any area of your life where you're releasing T-cells and antibodies?

Perhaps somebody does something that triggers an emotional response on the inside of you that has been there since childhood. If this person aligns with the information or disinformation you acquired when you were young, your rejection may have nothing to do with that person, but with those who have hurt you along the way.

You may be attacking what God sent to heal you. When you start rejecting people because of a hurt you've not been healed from, you will become an antibody. You could become anti-church or anti-small group, convincing yourself that you don't really fit anywhere, so you will reject them first and remain isolated and defeated.

God wants you to get into a body that can help you, heal you, and work with you. Refuse to let rejection define you. Learn from it.

Imagine if Walt Disney had allowed that editor's words to permeate and become his own. Could he have created all that he did if he had believed he had no creativity and little talent? He refused to be defined by the "nos" in his life, allowing him to step into all he was meant to be.

You can do the same. Don't let others' rejection define your trajectory. Don't let your fears reject what God has sent to enrich your life. Stop trying to fit into places God never destined you to fit into.

Jesus never hung around where he wasn't celebrated. He never tolerated rejection. Neither should you. Don't try to appease those who can't be appeased. Don't try to win the affections of someone who doesn't embrace all that you are. Go find people who will love, embrace, and celebrate you.

The Big Idea

When you know God's acceptance, you can endure man's rejection.
What rejection are you holding onto? How are you
letting it define you and shape your self-perception?
What are you rejecting today that God
has intended for your healing?

Prayer

*Lord, I thank You for knowing my every pain. Thank
you for setting me aside for a greater purpose. Help me
remember the truth about others' rejection and to abide
in Your unflinching, unconditional love for me.*

chapter 10

THE SEVENTH WAVE

Breaking the Limit of Fear

"Lord, if it's you," Peter replied, "tell me to come
to you on the water." "Come," He said.
—Matthew 14:29 (NIV)

Courage doesn't mean you don't get afraid.
Courage means you don't let fear stop you.
—Bethany Hamilton[23]

The water crusted my lips with a salty film as I watched the surfers ride the waves into shore.

"I can do that," I thought.

They were bodyboarding. Swim towards a wave, hold on tight, and ride it in. I could handle this.

So, I grabbed a bodyboard and started riding in on these little, tiny waves. My confidence grew with each one, and before long, I was eyeing the big ones—at least five-footers. Given my experience and skill

---

23 Bethany Hamilton (n.d.). AZQuotes.com. Retrieved on December 29, 2020, from AZQuotes. com. Website: https://www.azquotes.com/citation/quote/349301.

level, they might as well have been tidal waves. And then, I saw it. My wave was coming. It rushed at me, begging me to ride it all the way in.

I caught the wave, and just as I was getting balanced and feeling straight out of *Hawaii Five-O*, the tip of the board went down. And down. The board's nose disappeared under the surface of the water, pulling the board, with me attached, under the wave.

Suddenly, I was on the board's underside and was flipping head over heels over head over heels until I heard a noise that made my heart stop. The crack was a combination of a crunching, grinding sound that could only mean I was headed to a wheelchair for the rest of my life.

I contemplated my plight while praying there was a lifeguard nearby to pluck my limp, motionless body from the surf.

As I slipped below the surface, an image of Peter flashed in my head. Peter—the beloved, the man of great faith who looked a typhoon in the eyes, refocused on the man standing before him on the waves and took that fateful step out of the boat, onto the water … and walked! And then sank.

I wondered if Peter was embarrassed. Then I wonder if I would have had the bravado to get even as far as he did. It was amazing the number of things that I tossed around in my head as my body tossed around in the waves before landing on the sugar-soft sandy beach where I beheld the actual victim of that horrifying crunch.

To my delight and utter shock, my neck was intact, my legs were working, and the only injury was to my ego. My bodyboard had not fared so well. It turns out, it had sunk into the soft sand and snapped under the power of the water. Never had I been so equally delighted and embarrassed. A surfing legend, I was not—but I had a great story to tell.

WALKING ON WATER

We all know the Bible is filled with great stories, but few are as epic as that of the Savior walking on water. Of course, what pushes that one over the top is that Peter, His beloved follower, also jumped on the water and took off across the waves. While his aquatic jaunt was (shall we say) abbreviated, the fact that he left the boat at all to take on the maelstrom of the sea around him is commendable—even more so when you take in the whole scene.

This story is recounted somewhat differently in the various Gospels of the New Testament. The book of Matthew is the only one that tells the story of Peter walking out to Jesus. In Matthew 14, the story begins after Jesus has just fed the 5,000.

This was the 5,000 men who were in attendance to hear His teaching. We don't know how many women and children were also there. It is somewhat miraculous to feed four people three meals a day that provide sustenance and avoid sparking World War III in my house. Just think of potentially 20,000 people being fed from practically nothing. It was as though Jesus was priming the pump for miraculous expectations that day.

The story picks up in verse 22:

> Immediately, Jesus made the disciples get into the boat and go on ahead of him to the other side, while he dismissed the crowd. After he had dismissed them, he went up on a

mountainside by himself to pray. Later that night, he was there alone, and the boat was already a considerable distance from land, buffeted by the waves because the wind was against it. Shortly before dawn, Jesus went out to them, walking on the lake. When the disciples saw him walking on the lake, they were terrified. 'It's a ghost,' they said and cried out in fear. But Jesus immediately said to them: "Take courage! It is I. Don't be afraid." "Lord, if it's you," Peter replied, "tell me to come to you on the water." "Come," He said (Matthew 14:22-29, NIV).

If I were on a boat in the middle of the ocean (in a storm, no less), the chances are slim that I would be up on the top deck at all. Why? Because I know the basics of maritime safety, and I'm not crazy.

Several years ago, my wife and I went on a cruise. We boarded and were shuffled to our room. When I opened the door, half-expecting to see a terry cloth masterpiece awaiting us with two chocolates on the bed, I satiated my anticipation with a look out the window that kept the sea at a comfortable distance. We could see the millions of blue-green hues flicker under the sunlight, but what lay below the surface was just a hazy mystery that felt more comfortable to leave undiscovered.

Soon after we began realizing that there was no way the drawer space in this room was adequate, we were called to the on board ritual every modern maritime wanderer must undergo: the unveiling of the life jackets, lifeboats, and emergency procedures. The whole scenario was akin to an airline safety instruction presentation but elevated in some way. While the passengers were hoarded into a large area in a manner vaguely reminiscent of a pre-iceberg Titanic scene, the promise of the 24-hour buffet, soft-serve machine, and deck chairs somehow made all of these safety procedures seem superfluous. I was grateful for them, but they seemed unnecessary.

This was not so for the disciples aboard the ship in the middle of the Sea of Galilee. First off, this wasn't a two-in-the-afternoon-we-might-need-our-life-vests situation. This was a middle-of-the-night free-for-all panic room. The Sea of Galilee is seven miles across at its widest point, so they were likely three and a half miles from shore. That distance would be hard to swim in prime conditions. In the middle of a storm, next to impossible.

The disciples did not have a safety presentation, assigned life vests, and rescue vehicles stowed away "just in case." They were on their own, and they knew it.

Then the story changes drastically. The storm was surprising, but they had seen storms before. The geography of the Sea of Galilee makes it prone to sudden, violent storms. The weather was terrible, but they'd seen bad weather before. Now, as they fumbled with the ropes, the sails, and the torrents of water that crashed relentlessly on their deck, they looked out and saw a man coming toward them. This man was not in a boat. This man was not swimming. He was walking toward them on the water.

THE SEVENTH-WAVERS

I want to say that I'd be unfazed. Impressed, of course, but I'd love to know that I would know at a glance that this was my Savior. Who else could it be? After all, He had just fed thousands of people with five loaves of bread and two fish—of course He was walking on water!

I'd like to think I would react like Peter. It was as if the entire rest of the world faded away in an instant and all Peter could see was His Savior mastering the waves, conquering the winds, ready to receive him. So, in essence, he offered, "If it's really you, tell me to come."

And Jesus answered, "Come."

What did Peter do?

> Then Peter got down out of the boat, walked on the water and came toward Jesus. But when he saw the wind, he was afraid and, beginning to sink, cried out, "Lord, save me!"
> Immediately Jesus reached out his hand and caught him. "You of little faith," he said, "why did you doubt?"
> And when they climbed into the boat, the wind died down.
> Then those who were in the boat worshiped him, saying, "Truly you are the Son of God" (Matthew 14:29-33, NIV).

The long and short of it—Peter hopped out, took a few steps, then he sank right before uttering the shortest prayer in the Bible: "Lord, save me!"

Sure, he went down, but before he wiped out, he jumped out of the boat. He stood on the sea with his Savior.

Peter is representative of a type of people that have my admiration while mystifying me all at the same time. One group of people, when they see the waves rising, mentally recall the safety demonstration, make their way toward the life vests, and edge closer to the lifeboats. Safety first.

The second group has its eyes glued on the waves for entirely different reasons. Those people are watching to see how much bigger the waves will become. Then, they start edging toward their boards. Once the waves are massive, they're in the thick of it on the hunt for the biggest, fastest, baddest ride on the ocean.

These are the surfers.

I remember hanging out at the beach one day and happening to catch a couple of older surfers hanging out on their boards, watching the water, engage in what appeared to be a riveting tale of sand and sea. Hoping some of that surfer essence might rub off on me, I got closer until I could hear what they were saying. As I did, I could see the sun-bleached perfection of their hair that had known more salt than shampoo throughout their years and the leathery, baked-in permanent tan that is simply an impossibility for someone like me.

"How many was that?"

"I don't know. Why?"

"I'm waiting for the seventh wave."

Realizing I had no idea what they were talking about, I did what a Cincinnati boy out on the big blue ocean does: I googled it. What I found was an old surfer adage. While science vacillates on the validity of the claim, it has floated amongst surfer communities for years that waves come in sets of seven, with the seventh being the biggest and, obviously, the best.

Surfers live for the seventh wave.

In 2003, Bethany Hamilton was doing what she had done practically every day of her life—she was on the water, waiting for her wave. With her best friend beside her, the seasoned surfer (who was all of

13 at the time) suddenly felt a crushing blow that would strike terror in the heart of anyone. Within minutes, her world was upside down, she was floating on her battered board in a pool of red, and her arm was gone.

It wasn't broken.

It wasn't mangled.

It was gone.

Over the next couple of hours, she lost nearly 2/3 of her blood, underwent major surgery, and was forced into a life she had to relearn how to live because a shark had taken her arm.

With just one arm, day by day, she relearned how to get dressed, how to bathe, how to eat. In 26 days, she was back in the water, relearning how to surf. Within two years, she had won a national championship.

Bethany lives for the seventh wave.

I want to be a seventh wave type of person. I think, in some ways, Peter was a seventh wave kind of guy. For some reason, when the odds were against them all, literally in the middle of this furious storm, something within him not only told him that that ghost on the water was his Savior but, for whatever reason, he would be safer on the water with Jesus than on the boat without Him. That, my friend, is faith. Jesus was using this storm to grow Peter's faith. He wants to do the same with you and me. If you just trust Him in whatever storm you are in, you will grow through it.

Notice how I didn't say *survive*. Why? Because Jesus doesn't want us to just survive through our storms. He wants us to thrive. 2020 has been the year of one storm after another. There's no need to recount the list I'm sure runs through your head multiple times a day, but suffice it to say, it's been rough.

I've heard so many people say it's just going to get worse. The truth is that it might. Let's redefine worse. It might get stormier. The waves might get bigger. But here's the thing—the waves don't hide Jesus. They reveal Him.

When He was walking out to the men on the boat, they had no clue who it was! They thought it was a ghost! In their moment of crisis, these men who walked and talked and lived with Jesus Christ didn't recognize Him.

So, cut yourself some slack. It's hard to see Him sometimes. It can be hard to hear Him, but listen well. The waves are saying "sickness," but His voice is saying "healed." The waves are saying "broke," but His voice is saying "prosper." The waves are saying "fear," but He says "faith."

The waves say, "You are going to sink."

He says, "Step out and walk."

If you trust His voice, He's not going to let you fall. Even more, He's going to help you soar. Jesus did not need Peter to walk on water to survive that storm. Peter was just fine in the boat that was built for survival on the sea, just like the other guys, but Jesus wasn't interested in survival. He wanted Peter—you, me, all of us—to thrive.

People can survive. You can buy water and toilet paper and canned food and build a storm shelter and wear a life jacket, and you will, likely, survive. Surviving is what you can do. Thriving is what you need God to do. Surviving is playing it safe. Thriving is taking risks of faith and deciding not to fear what God can use to help you grow.

There are lots of sides to the coronavirus pandemic. It's up to all of us to be responsible and respectful and do what we can for the safety and well-being of others. However, it's also on us to look for opportunities to grow.

You may have been quarantined with your family without realizing that God was using this time together to make your family stronger than it's ever been. You may have been putting an education or an act of service off for years because you didn't have the time. While we're home, a lot of us have nothing but time.

This isn't to say to take the coronavirus lightly or to diminish the impact it is having worldwide. What I am saying is to look for Jesus in these waves. Listen for His voice.

When the disciples asked who it was, the scripture says He answered, "It is I." The literal translation of that phrase is, "I AM."

This is I AM who spoke to Moses and freed the Hebrews from the Egyptians. This is I AM who raises the dead, heals the sick, reverses the storms. This is I AM who feed the thousands. This is I AM who walks on water.

And I AM is coming for you. His arm is outstretched to you.

So, what are you going to do? Are you going to stay safe where you know you'll survive, or are you going to be like Peter, reach out your hand, and step out of the boat? If you are going to be like Peter, the chances are good that you might sink. And that's ok.

One of the most gratifying and relatable aspects of this story is that Peter was just as human as you or anyone else. By the grace of God, I am just as human as Peter—the man who walked on water with Jesus. It was also Peter—this man who began to sink while walking on water

THE SEVENTH WAVE

with Jesus. Why? The scripture says he began to notice the wind and the waves. He let his eyes look away from Jesus for just a moment, and at that moment, the waves felt bigger than the Word, and Peter began to go down.

When the waves start to rise in your life, don't let them wash away your experience. God has brought you through too much to assume that—this time—He won't pull through.

There was a woman who didn't have money to buy groceries. But every day, she would open her windows and praise God for providing. "You've done it before; I know You can do it again."

The man who lived next to her was an atheist, and one day, he'd just had it and thought, *I'll show her.*

So, he went to the grocery, bought a lot of food, stood in line, paid for the food, dropped it off at her front door, and then knocked before running to hide in the bushes. When she opened the door, she immediately began to praise God for providing yet again.

The man jumped out and said, "Ha! God didn't get those groceries for you. I did!"

The woman just said with a huge smile, "Thank you, God! Not only did you get me groceries, but you made the devil pay for them!"

God's not a God who bails on you. Not now. Not ever. Don't let your waves wash away what you know to be true.

Back to Peter. He was on the water. Can you imagine the moment? He was surely soaked through. His eyes were raw, but he could feel the warmth of the Master's hand in his. Then a massive wave came his way. The wind was relentless and, while he never let go, he let his eyes wander, and down he went.

Remember this: Don't ever be disappointed that Peter was the only disciple who sank in the Sea of Galilee. He was the only disciple who ever *walked* on the Sea of Galilee.

It's ok to stumble. Maybe you were dreaming big dreams and reaching goals and achieving things you'd never done before, and then the crisis hit, and now you feel like you're sinking.

It's ok.

Don't get discouraged, and don't allow the criticism of others to bring you down. There was only one person whose faith carried him out of the boat and onto the sea that night. If you are out of the boat, even if you are sinking, celebrate that you aren't sitting. I'd rather sink than sit. In a time of crisis, I'd rather talk faith and believe God for the best outcome than criticize others or decide that the worst is imminent. I'd rather do all I can to thrive than survive.

What did Peter do when he started to sink? He cried out, "Lord, save me!" It's the shortest prayer in the Bible, but it works! He didn't explain to Jesus what made him lose his faith, why things went wrong, or how he'll do better next time. His gut reaction was to cry out to Jesus, and Jesus' response was to save him. No questions asked. No conditions. He pulled him from the water and, once Peter was safe, He didn't condemn him. He simply asked, "Why did you doubt?"

It's a fair question: a hard question, but a fair one.

Did you know that over 60% of Americans are afraid of water? That fear leads to a lot of drownings. Why? Because the people who are scared of water never learn to swim.

It's essential to identify your fears and your weaknesses. It's smart to know your vulnerabilities. But don't leave it there. Don't stop with knowing why you can't or won't. Keep going until you can and do.

Waters are going to rise. Waves are going to crash. Make the most of your wave. Trust that it is not what is going to drown you. It is what will propel you.

Those surfers don't turn around at wave one or two. They face the sea, and they wait for the waves to grow and grow. Then they catch the biggest one they can, so they can ride higher and farther and faster than they ever have before. The water that should have taken you down, God can put under your feet and elevate you. He is a water-walking God, and we can be His water-walking disciples. He has put everything under His feet, which means everything is now under your feet.

Use your wave. Tell your story.

The Big Idea

Waves don't hide Jesus. They reveal Him.
What waves are you hiding from today? Do you
see Jesus in them? Can you hear His voice?
What is the last storm He pulled you through?
Will you trust Him to do it again?

Prayer

*Lord, I trust that You are using these waves to
make me better. I trust that You will send that
seventh wave, and it will make me thrive.*

chapter 11

THAT'S LIFE

Breaking the Limit of Predictability

And we know that for those who love God all things work together
for good, for those who are called according to his purpose.
—Romans 8:28 (ESV)

Life consists not in holding good cards but
in playing those you hold well.
—Josh Billings[24]

When Michelle found the lump, she didn't think much of it. She was still breastfeeding her five month old, and the mother of two had always been healthy. It was without much fear that she got the mammogram—but things then started to change.

The furtive glances between the nurses, the additional tests, and the eternally long wait for the doctor to go over results indicated that this might not be good news. When the doctor determined the need for a biopsy, Michelle and her husband waited with a sinking feeling.

---

24 Billings, J. BrainyQuote.com. Retrieved December 9, 2020, from BrainyQuote.com. Web site: https://www.brainyquote.com/quotes/josh_billings_161323.

And when the results confirmed an aggressive, nearly stage three breast cancer, the bottom dropped out of their lives.

Immediately, she began chemotherapy, the effects of which ravaged her body even more. Confined to her bed, she was consumed with thoughts of failure. Seeing little more than shame and guilt, it was hard for her to imagine what direction life would take.

THE CARDS YOU DRAW

In John 16:33, Jesus assures us of two things—life will be hard, but He's got it covered.

"In the world you will have tribulation. But take heart; I have overcome the world" (John 16:33b, ESV). It's comforting to know that Jesus has already won the war, but it's a little disconcerting when you realize you will still face your fair share of battles. That's life.

The board game, Life, is a stellar representation of the different circumstances and events that will ultimately shape how you live. As you move around the board, you draw various cards. One may send you on a certain career path that requires college or trade school. One card may say that you get a dog; another says you become parents of triplets. One says you'll live in a shack, and another card says you'll dwell in a mansion. Others say you lose your job, go bankrupt, win the lottery, get a promotion, or win a beauty contest.

You have to think strategically as you go since your choice determines the kind of cards you're going to draw for the rest of the game. Someone else may get a card that is like yours but leads to a wildly different outcome. Regardless, you'll likely get some great cards and some terrible cards.

Real life is much the same. You will be dealt blessings and some harsh blows. It's easy to lose one's footing, stray from the path, or simply disappear inside the pain of loss, rejection, or grief. It's in these moments of despair that Paul's words become a lifeline. Romans 8:28 unequivocally states that God works all things together for good.

He didn't say most things, some things, or a few things. He said *all* things.

It's not too difficult to read those words and understand them. For those who have experienced little, if any, tragedy or trauma, it's pretty easy to trust that everything is working together just as it should. It's another thing altogether to lean into that promise, believe it, and claim it when things are hard.

What happens if, one day, your doctor hands you a card that says, "You have cancer." Stings, doesn't it? You've never had to grapple with such a severe challenge, and suddenly you are facing the fight of your life.

Maybe your card is a pink slip. Your company may go under and take your salary, benefits, and security down with it.

Perhaps your card is one of unspeakable tragedy. Your card might say that your child dies. Now you have to cope with the most unnatural trauma one can experience. Children are supposed to bury their parents. Parents are never supposed to bury their children. That's not the way life works, right? Not quite.

As much as we like to pretend otherwise, we never know what cards life will deal us. You get a new job; you lose your job. You get a perfect bill of health; you have heart disease. You're going to have qua- druplets; sorry, you're not able to have children. You spend your whole life single; you get married, have two kids, a dog, and a white picket fence. You get married but go through a terrible divorce. You get mar- ried, but your spouse cheats on you and then puts it on social media.

How do you deal with a series of bad cards? You must reframe your approach to the game. Winning in life is not, nor has it ever been, about the cards which you are dealt. Your response to those cards determines victory. It doesn't matter what life gives you; what matters is how you respond. One pastor I know says life is 10 percent what happens to you and 90 percent how you react to it.

The challenge we typically face is the issue of control versus choice. It may seem that life has dealt you something awful that you can't control when you have controlled everything else up to that point. In reality, you have very little control over your life. You can come to church every time the doors are open and still go through the same storms as people who don't go to church. In the Sermon on the Mount, Jesus said, "For he makes his sun rise on the evil and on the good, and sends rain on the just and on the unjust" (Matthew 5:45, ESV).

Even when you're not in control, you always have a choice. Michelle couldn't control her diagnosis, but she chose to respond with dignity and faith. It would be easy for her to complain or question the fairness of life. She opted for a more hopeful frame of mind. She joined those who declare, "Even though life has dealt me this card, I'm going to choose to speak healing into my body. I'm going to choose to believe the promises of God. Even when things aren't going the way I want them to go, I can choose to worship. I can choose to praise."

In Psalm 118:24 (ESV), David said, "This is the day that the Lord has made; let us rejoice and be glad in it." David chose to rejoice. He didn't tell you what the day was bringing. He just said, "God made this day, and I'm going to choose to worship today." That's a choice you, too, can make every day.

LEARNING FROM HISTORY

There is no shortage of unfortunate life cards being distributed throughout Scripture. However, Hagar's story is particularly compelling given that the ramifications of the hand which she was dealt still resonate today. Hagar's son, Ishmael, would become the father of the Arab nations, meaning much of today's global conflict can trace its roots to this story and the characters within.

As the story unfolds, it's clear that the decisions and their resulting consequences were birthed (literally) from disobedience—namely Abraham's and Sarah's (who were earlier known as Abram and Sarai). Despite the less-than-righteous circumstances, God's hand and blessing remained on Hagar and Ishmael. Ishmael's descendants became a great nation because the blessing of God was on their lives.

Hagar's life wasn't easy, and certainly not one you and I would have chosen. While we don't know the exact details of her backstory, suffice it to say that Hagar's daily existence was difficult. When she was young, like so many others, she became a slave in Egypt. Hagar was traded from owner to owner to owner until, one day, a new caravan came into Egypt. They didn't look like the other Egyptians and were led by a man named Abraham. At some point, Hagar's ownership was transferred to Abraham.

As the story progresses, God promised Abraham a son and descendants as plentiful as the sands on the seashore and the stars in the heavens. Then, 10 years go by—10 years with no son and no descendants.

Now, you would probably concede that not every promise from God pans out the next day—or even the next year. I've heard that you have to hold on to a dream for five years before you see it.

Abraham held on for five years. And then five more. And all of a sudden, he was in his late 90s, Sarah was in her late 80s, and the math and calendar and biological clocks were not lining up. Abraham was discouraged. Sarah was discouraged. More than that, she was filled with shame. In that culture and era, a wife who failed to produce a child had failed as a wife. She felt the eyes of judgment all around her. She knew the gossip and rumor mills were filled with her name and her shortcomings.

Eventually, it became too much. She was done waiting. She told herself that maybe God's promise didn't include her. Perhaps Abraham was to have a child with someone … anyone. Her internal dialogue led her to a drastic decision. The Genesis story recounts: "Sarai said to Abram, 'Behold now, the Lord has prevented me from bearing children. Go into my servant; it may be that I shall obtain children by her'" (Genesis 16:1–2, ESV). What was Abraham's response? "And Abram listened to the voice of Sarai" (v. 2).

Can you imagine having such a conversation? Bear in mind— this was common. It was not unusual for a surrogate to be used if a woman couldn't have children. It made sense, culturally, for Sarah to urge her husband to go into her servant, Hagar, so that she could bear his child in her place.

As logical a solution as this seemed to be, you and I can both see the writing on the wall. Decisions like this inevitably result in unintended, often unpleasant consequences. Sarah knew what the Lord had said and promised, yet she listened to the voices, whispers, and common practices around her, which leads us to this big idea: Just because something sounds good to someone else doesn't mean it's right for you. You will spend your entire life surrounded by people and their opinions.

Grantland Rice, legendary sports columnist, said, "A wise man makes his own decisions; an ignorant man follows public opinion.[25]" When you find yourself in a moment of despair or confusion, be mindful of your sources of advice and guidance. It's like the person who's been divorced three times advising a single person, or the person who's never been married advising a married person. It doesn't make sense. People can't know what they're talking about if they've never experienced it. Know where your advice is coming from. Do your advisors have relationships with God? Do they hear God's voice? Have their words proven correct in the past?

These may seem like trivial points, but the consequences—good and bad—of advice heeded or ignored are real, and will inevitably impact people beyond you. Sarah had a problem, and she devised a solution based on others' input and cultural norms. She couldn't bear a child, so she found someone who could, and a baby was born. That

---

25 Rice, Grantland. (n.d.). BrainyQuote.com. Retrieved December 28, 2020, from BrainyQuote. com. Web site: https://www.brainyquote.com/quotes/grantland_rice_118347.

baby and his descendants continue to be associated with ongoing conflict and unrest today.

Somewhere, this solution went off the rails. It didn't hold up. Today, if a woman were unable to have kids and brought a friend to her husband to take her place, you would say, "Now what?" But in Sarah and Hagar's day, it was culturally common. It was acceptable. It was logical. But here's the thing about culture—things change. The Word of God never changes. When it comes to making critical decisions, you stand to lose a lot if you judge acceptability in terms of culture rather than the Word of God.

A HAGAR MOMENT

Abraham and Sarah's decision birthed a solution that came with a lot of baggage. In doing so, they forced Hagar into a situation over which she had no control. Through decisions and choices not of her making, Hagar became pregnant. She entered Abraham's tent as a maid and walked out as a mom. Her life would never be the same.

Chances are, you too have carried the weight of something you didn't choose. Maybe you're raising your kids' kids. Maybe your spouse walked out, and you are shouldering all the bills and all the parenting. What was supposed to have been a team effort is now a solo endeavor. Whatever the cause, your life has now changed forever in a way you didn't want, didn't seek, and didn't deserve.

If this sounds like you, you've experienced what I call a Hagar moment. Hagar moments happen when someone assumes God didn't do everything He was supposed to do. Said person then crafts a back-up plan to cover for God. He or she becomes impatient, and instead of waiting on God, decides to play God. So, that person says, "Fine, God, if you're not going to do it, I'll go out and do it myself."

Sarah grew impatient. She grew tired of waiting for God's promise, so she stepped into His role and tried to jump-start God's promises to them. Hagar became collateral damage in the wake of Sarah's lack of faith, and as is so often the case when people decide to play God, it didn't end well.

Soon, the tables turned. Hagar, the victim, became Hagar, the mother-to-be—right in front of the woman who never had been. As her baby bump grew, she mastered the art of selfies and the reverse photobomb. Every photo she captured, she made sure Sarah was in the background.

Why? Did she want to make Sarah jealous? Well, if that was her plan, she succeeded. Sarah still couldn't conceive, and Hagar wouldn't let her forget it. As her baby grew, so too did Hagar's pride and Sarah's resentment. Sarah started persecuting Hagar. The Bible says she dealt with her treacherously. Eventually, Hagar couldn't take it anymore, so she ran away. She ended up in the wilderness because she couldn't handle the blessing.

Can you? Once life starts handing you cards of good fortune—new cars, new jobs, new relationships, etc.—do you notice a shift in your personality? Do you still hang with the same people, or has your good fortune made you better than they are? If the answer for the latter is "yes," first and foremost, thanks for being honest with yourself. Second, you're not the first, and you won't be the last to behave and interact with others in such a manner. Third, don't ever forget where

God brought you from. Never forget that, without His grace, you could be broken and alone. The same principle applies to the good cards you are dealt in life. It's not the card that matters—it's how you respond to it that determines your character.

CHOICES AND CONTROL

Hagar's story is a masterclass in choices and control. Nearly every circumstance that impacted Hagar was beyond her control. When life deals us a heavy blow that we can't control, it can blindside us because we think we've controlled everything else up to that point.

We are wrong! We haven't been controlling anything—not even a little bit. Not our kids, spouse, or finances!

The Bible says that it rains on the just and the unjust. Hard things happen to those who go to church everyday just as often as those who have never darkened the door. The truth is that not only are you not in control now, you have never been. However, while you don't have control, you do have a choice.

You can't control the doctor's diagnosis, but you can choose how you will respond to it. And you have options. You can choose to complain about life or blame your family genetics. You can choose to bitterly accept that this is just the way life is.

Or you can choose to speak healing into your body. You can choose to believe God's promises. Even when things aren't going the way you want them to go, you can choose to worship and praise.

Remember that David said, "This is the day the Lord has made. I will rejoice and be glad in it."

He didn't know what the future held. He simply said, "The day belongs to the Lord, and I will praise Him. Even if this day doesn't go well, God always goes well."

Life will not always play fair. It's going to be hard, and the competition will be fierce. It will appear as if everyone else is trying to beat the game before you do, to cross that finish line first, regardless of the casualties inflicted along the way.

I heard a story about a group of frogs going through the woods. They came to a pit they didn't see, and two frogs fell in. They just happened to grab the side and started jumping, trying to get out of the pit. But the sides were slippery, and escape seemed impossible. The bottom of the pit was a death sentence. All the other frogs crowded around the mouth of the pit, telling them, "It's too steep, too slippery. You'll never make it."

One of the frogs got tired, gave up, and fell to the bottom of the pit. The other kept jumping. And jumping. And jumping. All the while, the other frogs were yelling at him to just give up.

Finally, he worked his way up and out. Exhausted and out of breath, the surviving frog was soon surrounded by the others who asked why he didn't listen to them.

"We told you to give up," they said.

"I'm sorry," he responded. "I'm hard of hearing. I thought you were all cheering for me."

Just like the frog, you're going to face a lot of people who are not cheering you on to victory. But when the haters arise, just remember that there must be a reason they're hating on you. You must be getting close to the top, close to your blessing.

THE FUEL OF CRITICISM

If the level of criticism and backlash you face does indeed correlate with the proximity of your blessing, then Hagar's was within arm's reach. Sarah's anger had driven her into the wilderness, where the angel of the Lord found her and asked her to do the unthinkable—go back to Sarah. More precisely, the angel told her to submit to Sarah and that the Lord would multiply her descendants "so that they cannot be numbered for multitude" (Genesis 16:10, ESV).

Hagar had to have felt some mixed emotions. The promise of multiple descendants was appealing, but it came at a price. She had to go back to the woman who had treated her so cruelly.

Have you ever been in a place where they did wrong, but God corrects you? They lied. They cheated. They betrayed you, and God rebukes you. You probably want to say, "What? What are you watching? God, did you change channels for a moment because they're the ones who owe me an apology."

Why does God do this? Perhaps it's because criticism and correction are the fuel you need to move closer to your promise.

I was in a vocal class in Bible college, and there wasn't a single thing I could do without the teacher yelling at me. I couldn't even blink! Everything I did was greeted with, "Eric. Stop, Eric. Eric. Eric." It was like she did nothing during the whole class but watch me.

Whenever I sang, it was, "You're singing wrong, Eric. You're standing wrong. Eric. You're holding your voice wrong. Eric, don't sing like that. Eric, don't breathe like that. Eric, don't do that."

Finally, I walked up to her and said, "Why are you always picking on me?"

She said, "Because you've got a talent the other kids don't have. I'm harder on you because I see more in you! I'm picking on you because there's so much inside of you that the enemy wants to take and destroy. And I want to make sure nothing holds you back."

BLESSINGS IN THE HARD PLACES

Most of us aren't overly fond of the idea of submission, which also means to acquiesce or surrender. God sent Hagar back to a hard place, a painful place, a place of persecution. He also promised that if she returned to the pain, He would birth a promise within. It couldn't have been easy for her. It's not easy for anyone.

You might be ready to walk away from a difficult situation or relationship because it's hard, but God tells us to submit, to stay in the painful places, so He can birth promises within us. As uncomfortable as it may seem, God says, "Submit. This isn't about them. This is about you and Me. What I'm doing in you is greater than anything they can do to you."

He sent her back, telling her to submit and go back to the pain for Him to birth a promise. You may want to walk out of a marriage right now because it's just not easy being married. God says you need to submit, and you need to stay in this because you'll never birth the promise that He has for you unless you submit and do what He's asking you to do. You'll never be blessed until you submit to the thing to which God is calling you to submit.

God is more interested in your submission than your solutions. He wants to teach you. He wants to heal you. He wants to birth His promise within you, and you can trust that the promise will always be bigger than the pain—a truth I have come to know intimately.

LEARNING FROM THE MASTER

I went to a Bible college which was also part of the church I was attending. Just after completing my studies, a leader within the church came to me one day and said, "Eric, we want to offer you a job as an alternate praise and worship leader. You will also teach praise and worship in the Bible college. When needed, we want you to lead worship in the sanctuary."

This was everything I had worked for. This particular church was huge, with about 6,500 people on an average Sunday. I immediately pictured myself on that platform, spotlights on me, thousands of people listening to me sing. I'll never forget the voice of God in my head, saying, "Go home."

"But God ... 6,500 people! Millions watching on television. Only 350 at home. I don't want to go home. I want to take this job, God. This is what I want."

"Go home."

So, I looked at the church leader and said, "Thank you, but I need to go home."

I went home, and I had all these ideas, and my dad, the pastor, didn't want to do any of them. I remember thinking, "Man, I could be up in that huge church right now, up there singing in front of 6,500 people. God, why did You call me back here? I could have been fulfilling my calling in front of all these multitudes of people."

Slowly, in my lament, I began to realize that God had taken me home because there were things my father needed to teach me—lessons I could never have learned on that platform in front of thousands of people.

I trailed him everywhere. We would go to funerals, and my dad would say, "Eric, get a song ready. You're going to sing."

"But there's no music."

"Sing a cappella."

In moments like this, I learned how to care for those who were grieving. I followed Dad to the hospital, where he would hold a patient's hand and pray for him or her. I learned how to care for people when they're sick and how to support a family when their loved one is taking his or her final breath.

I learned Hagar-type humility, too. When people wronged us, my father would tell me, "Eric, call and apologize to them."

I'd say, "No. That's where I draw the line, Dad."

And he'd repeat, "You pick up the phone, call them, and apologize."

Dad taught me it's not worth it to go through life holding a grudge toward people. Forgive them and move along. He also taught me to keep my cool in the pulpit. He taught me to preach life into the congregation, to preach the gospel unto them, and to preach the message of salvation to them.

These lessons were priceless, pivotal, and the very reason I'm doing what I am today. I had a choice to make. I chose to say, "Yes, God. I'll submit, and I'll do it your way."

THE BREAKING AND THE MAKING

Hagar had a choice to make, too. While everything around her was out of control, she chose to submit. She returned to the hard place. She went back to Sarah and gave birth to Ishmael. Before long, God fulfilled His promise to Abraham. Sarah conceived and delivered Isaac, and then, little boys did what little boys usually do. Ishmael made fun of Isaac.

As the parent of an ousted nursery student, I understand the frustration. Kim took our 1½-year-old son to the nursery, and within five minutes, he had pulled hair, pinched some kids, and bit a couple of people. You know, boys being boys, and childcare workers being responsible childcare workers, they requested that we remove him from the nursery.

Sarah essentially did the same. She didn't like that Ishmael was picking on her son and told Abraham to make both Hagar and Ishmael leave. Abraham wasn't thrilled about this idea, given that Ishmael was his son too, but God assured him that he should do what Sarah has asked him to do.

Enter Hagar's understandable confusion. She had listened to God and returned to this unpleasant place years before, and now she was being made to leave again. It didn't make sense. I can imagine what that conversation between Hagar and God must have been like:

"If it's time for me to go, God, why did I ever have to come back?"

"I wanted to see if you would submit. There were things you needed to learn. You had become stubborn and prideful. You had allowed favor to make you arrogant. You were sent back to break the pride out of you, to break the arrogance and jealousy out of you. You were sent back to be broken. In time, I won't be just breaking you; I'll be remaking you."

Sound familiar? Hagar's story is my story. I'd venture to guess it's your story. We all encounter seasons that are necessarily created for breaking and refining. In Jeremiah, we read how the potter remakes a broken vessel. He grinds it down to powder and then begins to remake it.

In Genesis 21, Hagar and Ishmael are broken. They have been sent away into the wilderness, Ishmael is dying of thirst, and Hagar is spent. She's holding a deck of cards she didn't ask for and doesn't know what to do with. In that moment of brokenness, surrender, and submission, God calls out and says He will make Ishmael into a great nation, and then He opens her eyes so she can see the well that's been in front of her the whole time.

What God did for Hagar and Ishmael in the wilderness is what He is ready and eager to do for you, regardless of the cards that life has dealt to you. Where did Ishmael come from? Someone else's bad decision. Why was Hagar sent out into the wilderness? Someone else's bad decision.

The point is that it doesn't matter how bad the decisions are that have placed you where you are today. It doesn't matter how dire the circumstances that have put you in the hospital or on a waiting list or alone as a single parent. God can use all of those things to bless you, teach you, and demonstrate His love to you. Romans 8:28 tells us He works all things—even the most painful ones—for good.

When Michelle found that lump, received her diagnosis, and was lying in bed sick from chemo, she found herself playing with a deck of cards she didn't ask for, and she didn't want. But she chose to trust that God would do what He said He would do. She chose to trust that all the pain would eventually lead to blessing.

You can't predict the cards you'll draw or craft the circumstances of your life and the people in it. You have as much control over most of the people and places in your life as you do controlling whether the sky will be filled with sunshine or rain clouds. But you do have a choice. You always have a choice, and your life will eventually become a collective of those choices.

When you're facing a diagnosis, a heartache, a loss, think of Hagar. God didn't arbitrarily put her in dangerous or uncomfortable places. He continually gave her opportunities to choose to grow, discard her arrogance or pride, and become capable of receiving His blessing. He spent years breaking and making her into the mother of a great nation—not to punish her, but to bless her.

He is not breaking you down today to punish you. He is using today and the circumstances you encounter to prepare you, better you, prime you to receive His blessing, and build a life—a life that enables others to do the same.

The Big Idea

The promise is always bigger than the pain. What cards has life handed you that you didn't expect and aren't sure what to do with? What choices can you make today to loosen your grip on the pain and move closer to the promise of His blessings? Are you ready to believe that the life He has for you is bigger than the pain of today?

Prayer

God, I will submit to doing life Your way. Help me learn what I need to learn, lose what I need to lose, and trust that even in the breaking, You are making something greater out of me.

chapter 12

FINDING YOUR GREATNESS

Breaking the Limit of Ordinary

*"Truly, I say to you, unless you turn and become like children,
you will never enter the Kingdom of Heaven. Whoever humbles
himself like this child is the greatest in the Kingdom of Heaven."*
—Matthew 18:3-4 (ESV)

*"You were designed for accomplishment, engineered for
success, and endowed with seeds of greatness."*
—Zig Ziglar[26]

O ne day, a little girl was born with her head attached to her shoulders, blind in one eye, no left forearm, missing fingers, and puck feet. Her father took one look at her in the delivery room and left her mother forever.

---

26 Zig Ziglar Quotes. (n.d.). BrainyQuote.com. Retrieved December 29, 2020, from BrainyQuote. com Website: https://www.brainyquote.com/quotes/zig_ziglar_724588.

Another little girl was born to addicts who couldn't care for any of their children. Thrust into foster care at an early age, the girl was eventually adopted and began a new life without her mom and dad.

Both little girls were born into hardship. Neither had any pedigree to speak of. They didn't come from money, and they didn't experience the love and support from their biological parents that they needed. According to the rules of life, little girls like this don't get very far. More than likely, wherever they do end up, they'll be there alone. The world says these little girls aren't great.

The world is wrong.

The world has had it wrong for a long time. In Matthew, we see the disciples asking Jesus about the ranking system of heaven. Jesus' response was to take a child and place him in the middle of these glory-seeking grown men and say, "Truly, I say to you unless you turn and become like children, you will never enter the kingdom of heaven. Whoever humbles himself like this child is the greatest in the kingdom of heaven" (Matthew 18:3-4, ESV).

In a culture that values strength, possessions, and maturity, the greatness of heaven is practically an inversion of what we have been taught to pursue and prize, which leads to some critical questions. *What is greatness? Can anyone achieve it?* Zig Ziglar said, "You were designed for accomplishment, engineered for success, and endowed with seeds of greatness." In other words, everyone has the seeds of greatness within them, but those seeds must be nourished and cultivated for greatness to spring forth.

When you think about greatness and limitless living, it's hard to overlook the Olympics. For centuries, the best of the best have competed in testing the limits of human endurance, precision, and accomplishment. These athletes are the pinnacle of commitment and talent—greatness.

Every two years, my wife and I love watching the opening ceremonies, the lighting of the torch, the presentation of the athletes, and the different flags and cultures from all over the world coming together in the name of sportsmanship and competition. It's as though the best of humanity is on display.

But, let us not forget one of the most significant components of the Olympic experience—the commercials. A few years back, Adidas put out a great ad campaign featuring the top athletes in their latest, greatest gear. Naturally, Nike had to compete, so they released a campaign of their own that was similar—featuring athletes in Nike attire—but different, in that these athletes were unknowns.

These were the kids on the soccer field, the little boy on the diving board at the community pool, and the kid shooting baskets in the backyard. These athletes were you and me to a degree. From my perspective, apart from being brilliant, this ad campaign answered the fundamental question of what it is to be great and who can claim the title. The long and short of it is that greatness can come from anywhere or anyone—with a significant caveat—you have got to earn it.

The people in these ads were everyday people from Everywhere, USA, but each one of them was in motion, committed, and determined. It wasn't just the characters in the ads that stuck in my mind. The writers behind this campaign were on fire. Each ad featured a tag line about greatness that was more than an excellent t-shirt logo. Over the years, I've often rolled these nuggets of wisdom around in my subconscious, unwittingly allowing them to permeate my thoughts and personal understanding of greatness. Allow me to share.

GREATNESS IS SCARY UNTIL IT ISN'T

By in large, the first time you do something is scary. Giving a speech, scaling a climbing wall, participating in the Olympics, or, in my case, rappelling down from the giant obstacle course that occupies an unassuming presence beside one of those clog-your-arteries, more-butter-please, Southern homestyle restaurants in the great adventurer's wilderness of Pigeon Forge, Tennessee.

The course was unnecessarily high and long and had two ways out. Go back or rappel down from the highest point. Championed by Saige, my nine-year-old daughter and wilderness expert, I had no choice but to complete the course and to exit via the way of greatest danger, or so it seemed from three stories above the concrete ground. I'm pretty sure there was a shift in oxygen levels in the air due to the altitude. Either that or something else was making me dizzy, nauseous, and lightheaded all at the same time. Talk about great family fun!

When I reached the point of no return, the unassuming and remarkably unconcerned obstacle course worker held out a slender belt to which my harness would attach. All about one-inch wide, this belt looked more suitable for closing a bag of cereal or lifting a bundle of feathers than supporting the weight of a full-grown man.

Masking my true feelings, I did that nervous laugh and asked, "So this thing holds how much? I'm six-three, 235 pounds, give or take. Just want to make sure it can take me!"

Without a second thought, he responded, "You're good. This thing holds up to 300 pounds … I think."

Hesitating, I first thought, "That 'I think' was unnecessary."

Then I did some quick math in my head, considering the g-forces at work, how they would multiply my weight, how it would increase due to the rapid acceleration on the long descent. A lot was going on.

"Whoa," I said, eloquently presenting my case. "Given the g-force and the distance, 235 and 300 aren't that far apart."

"You're good," was the response.

Then the battle began in force. My legs carried me to the edge. Then my head told me, *Bro, you can't do this. Your legs are fully encased in Jell-O, and you're going to need them beyond this moment right here and now. You will also need the rest of your body and your faculties. A brain injury would greatly complicate your ministry efforts, that is concrete, and you do not bounce.*

Then, I heard the voice of my fearless leader and inspiration. From the crowd that had continuously grown throughout my now-extended stint on the jumping platform, I heard Saige's voice yelling, "Dad! C'mon! You're holding up the line."

Wow. Truly the wind beneath my wings.

Then the counting started. For whatever reason, people assumed that they could will me down with the anthem of a countdown. It was like a Gregorian chant from down below.

"Three, two, one."

"Three, two, one."

For whatever reason, they always just started at three. I looked to the crowd below, and, in response to their cheers, I offered, "You can count all day long. I will go when I am good and ready."

I don't know if it was the smell of butter wafting up from the cookery down below or the raw call of the wild inside of me, but after a time that I have hence decided is unimportant to this story, I leaped from the safety of the platform into the air, gently lowering to the ground below in all of three to four seconds.

My mission was over. My task was complete. I had achieved greatness (which can be relative), and it was terrifying. But now, I know there is not a single rappelling wall of no more than three stories off the ground that can defeat me.

Nike was right—greatness is scary until it isn't.

SOMETIMES, GREATNESS ISN'T PRETTY

I've never been one of those people who can run a mile with minimal sweat, no discoloration; you know the type. When I work out for nearly any length of time at almost any level of effort, my face turns what appears to be a grossly unhealthy and unnatural shade of red, and every layer of clothes I am wearing is soaked in sweat. You wouldn't be out of line to worry about my health.

But, according to Nike (thank you, Nike), that's just greatness at work. With the tagline, "Greatness isn't always pretty," they paved the way for people like me to feel triumphant at the gym even if we look like a medical crisis in process.

It's also pertinent to one of the most astonishing races in the 2012 Olympics. Allyson Felix is one of the most decorated female runners. She had won five gold medals on the women's relay team, claimed the gold in the 200-meter and a silver in the 400-meter in 2016. She's unnaturally skilled and mind-boggling to watch.

In one race of the 2012 games, she was heavily favored to win, and it looked like a sure thing until the very end. At that moment, the runner from the Bahamas dove across the finish line, just a hair ahead of Felix. The crowd exploded, social media exploded, and it seemed like everyone had something to say about this monumental dive to gold. To quell the growing discontent, the commentators came on the air and said, "We just want to clarify the rules. It doesn't matter how you cross the line; it just matters who crosses the line first."

Greatness requires sacrifice, a lot of hard, grueling work, and is more often dirty, sweaty, and unattractive than it is pretty.

I'll never forget the 1996 Summer Olympics and the Magnificent Seven. For years, Russia had dominated women's gymnastics, and this was the first team that was poised to take the all-around gold. It all came down to one last vault from Kerri Strug. The vault itself was a complicated, high-scoring element. On the first of her two passes, she hit the mat and just crumpled. No one knew it at the time, but she had severely sprained her ankle and torn two ligaments.

Mathematically, she had to land her second vault on her feet for her team to clinch the gold. Grimacing, she walked to the end of the runway, took off, and briefly landed her vault on both feet before hopping to her uninjured leg. Then she collapsed. She earned a 9.712

and was in so much pain, she had to be carried to the podium by the USA coach.

As the team recalled their dramatic moments from 1996 after 20 years, Strug said: "I'll remember the moment on the podium forever. I definitely had some contrasting emotions. I thought I was going to look like Mary Lou Retton [1984 gold medalist], and instead, I'm crying. I have no pants on!"[27]

Greatness isn't always pretty. It requires sacrifice and pain, but for those who achieve it, it's not the aesthetic of the moment that matters.

GREATNESS ISN'T DECIDED BY JUDGES

Watching just about any sport today would logically lead you to conclude that judges are a decisive factor in greatness. Then again, turn on the TV or your phone or computer, and good luck avoiding a reality contest of some kind. They are everywhere. It's as though we are addicted, as a collective culture, to competition, ranking, and conquering.

Nike had the foresight to see that rank, place, or judges' comments don't have any determination on what makes someone great. Believe it or not, there's biblical precedence for this. In several Gospels, the story is recounted of a prostitute who learned where Jesus was having dinner with his disciples and some of the Pharisees.

---

27 Meyers, D. (2016) "What Really Happened Before and After Kerri Strug's Famous Vault." *ELLE.* Retrieved from: https://www.elle.com/culture/a38123/oral-history-of-the-magnificent-seven/.

Already, you can see a storm brewing—prostitute, Pharisees, disciples, Jesus. Hang on tight.

The woman learned where Jesus was, showed up with an alabaster jar of perfume, began anointing His feet with it, and wiped them with her hair. What a moment this must have been! First, this was no discount store perfume. This type of "ointment," as it is called in the book of Matthew, could have cost around 300 pence. At the time, a day's wage was about one pence, give or take. So, this woman was using almost an entire year's salary to anoint Jesus.

Matthew 26:8-9 (ESV) says, "And when the disciples saw it, they were indignant, saying, 'Why this waste? For this could have been sold for a large sum and given to the poor.'" Just for context, the very next scene is Judas asking the chief priests how much they would give him for turning Jesus in.

Back to dinner. The Pharisees and the disciples found nothing great about what this woman was doing. They were eager to dole out criticisms and judgment. In Mark's account, the clapbacks are even harsher.

"Why was the ointment wasted like that? For this ointment could have been sold for more than three hundred denarii and given to the poor. And they scolded her" (Mark 14:4-5, ESV).

Jesus' response is epic. "Leave her alone. Why do you trouble her? She has done a beautiful thing to me" (Mark 6:6, ESV).

Luke records Jesus using a hypothetical. He asks the men if two people owe a debt to a moneylender and both debts are canceled, who will love the lender more—the one with the larger or smaller debt?

"Simon answered, 'The one, I suppose, for whom he canceled the larger debt.' And He said to him, 'You have judged rightly'" (Luke 7:43, ESV).

Jesus then walked them through the logic:

"Do you see this woman? I entered your house; you gave me no water for my feet, but she has wet my feet with her tears and wiped them with her hair. You gave me no kiss, but from the time I came in, she has not ceased to kiss my feet. You did not anoint my head with oil, but she has anointed my feet with ointment. Therefore, I tell you, her sins, which are many, are forgiven—for she loved much. But he who is forgiven little loves little" (Luke 7:44-47, ESV).

Jesus then forgave the woman, to which everyone responded with shock asking who this man was that He would forgive sins. They didn't even know who Jesus was—but she did.

The bottom line is this: This woman did a great thing. The people around her chose not to see it. In the end, however, it was Jesus' decision, Jesus' judgment that not only mattered, but it was also correct.

It's far too easy to judge other people based on pretty much anything and everything. Social media has ballooned the business of gossip to unprecedented proportions. Most people would rather sit behind a screen, doling out judgment on others who are doing something, but here's the truth—great people don't have time to gossip. I love a quote that's often attributed to Eleanor Roosevelt: "Great minds discuss ideas. Average minds discuss events. Small minds discuss people."[28] People of greatness don't have time to gossip.

28 Eleanor Roosevelt Quotes. (n.d.). BrainyQuote.com. Retrieved January 7, 2021, from BrainyQuote.com Web site: https://www.brainyquote.com/quotes/eleanor_roosevelt_385439.

GREATNESS ISN'T BORN
GREATNESS IS MADE

You are not great because of who your parents were, nor are you blocked from greatness because of who your parents weren't. Greatness—your entire future—is determined by choices, not because of where you were or weren't born. Joshua said, "Choose this day, whom you will serve" (Joshua 24:15, ESV).

Every day, I face a litany of choices, all of which will impact the quality of my day. I can press snooze, or I can get up when my phone tells me to. I can load up on doughnuts and anticipate a sugar crash, or I can eat something sensible and have sustained energy throughout the day. I can also be kind, compassionate, and patient, or I can snap at people, lose my temper, and be indifferent.

While there are lots of things I can't control in life, these things I can. And it's the choices—the small ones and the big ones—that will lead me to success or a spiral. Jim Collins, who wrote *Good to Great*, said, "Greatness is not a function of circumstance. Greatness is largely a matter of conscious choice."

I recently revisited the book of Esther and was stunned at how pertinent her story is to me, and probably to you, right here and now. Esther was Jewish. She was born and raised by her uncle, Mordecai, who was also Jewish.

One day, the king kind of put out an "all call" for the most beautiful women to replace his first wife. Esther was among them, and, with outer beauty matching her inner beauty, she won the crown.

A series of events put into motion a plan to annihilate all the Jews in the kingdom. Esther's uncle begged her to talk to the king to spare her race. Small problem. First, the king was not aware of her lineage. Second, if anyone went to see him sans an invite, he or she could be killed. He was not keen on unexpected guests.

She explained her very rational concerns to Mordecai, who told her that if she did nothing, someone else would, but she probably would not make it out alive. If she did something, God would bless her and spare her people.

This was not an easy decision. I can only imagine how terrified she must have been and how torn she must have felt between the place of her birth and the station to which she had been appointed. Even so, she somehow found the strength, and she showed up for her people. The king listened to her, and the Jewish people were spared.

Esther was not born into a household whose members would ever see the king—much less influence him. It didn't matter. Her moment of greatness came to fruition because she determined not to let her circumstances write her story.

Esther is not the only woman wearing a crown who has defied her beginnings. The little girl who was born with severe deformities continued to experience excruciating rejection and abuse for much of her life. Today, that little girl is all grown up. Her name is Ellie, and she greets each day with a smile on her face, expectation in her heart, and from time to time, a tiara on her head. Called "Queen" by those who know and love her, Ellie has experienced God's restoration in every part of her life.

After her 21-year marriage ended, Ellie was given a house and some land to call home by a family member. In years to come, she would meet and marry a wonderful man who treats her like the beautiful daughter of God that she is.

"God turned my ashes into beauty," she says with a smile.

Over time, she came to trust that her earthly birth had no bearing upon the blessings from her Heavenly Father.

"He began to show me that I wasn't a mistake, that I was knit together in my mother's womb just the way I am for a purpose—to reveal His glory. When you experience all the difficulties I have, the enemy would like you to be hopeless. However, I feel that hope is exactly the thing I have to offer to others."

Ellie wasn't born into greatness. Her spirit, drive, affection, grace, capacity to forgive, and eagerness to love truly make her one of the greatest of all time, which, oddly enough, is said regularly about the second little girl born into a world of hurt to parents who couldn't move past their addictions to love and care for their daughter.

Her grandparents stepped in, adopted her, and loved, nurtured, and supported her on a journey that would make her the most decorated female gymnast of all time. Simone Biles wasn't born into greatness. The love of others, her belief in herself, and her tireless dedication to her passion have converged for her to make a mark on history as the greatest.

When you think about your origin story, would you say you were destined for greatness? Or ... not so much? The truth is that you can start making decisions today to set your feet on a path to something spectacular. It won't be an easy journey. It will require sacrifice and a willingness to commit to a path of greatness.

Those who become great are teachable. They are correctable. They don't assume they know the most or perform the best—that would make them complacent, and complacency and greatness cannot coexist.

Strive to be a lifelong learner. Never assume you know everything there is to know about anything. Stay hungry for knowledge, be intentional to acquire wisdom, and put yourself in the company of those who have walked the road to greatness before you. Pay attention. Learn all you can. Seek opportunities to improve, enhance, or elevate your skills, your relationships with Christ and with others, and your decisions.

Proverbs 10:17 (NKJV) says, "He who keeps instruction is in the way of life, but he who refuses correction goes astray."

There is a stark difference between talent and teachability. Some who are born with a great deal of talent, but aren't teachable, will crash and burn. Others who may not be born with natural talent, but are teachable, willing, and eager to learn, will soar. When it comes to a talented person versus a teachable spirit, teachability wins every time. Whereas we gauge greatness in glory, God determines greatness by one's humility of heart and generosity of spirit.

ARRIVE UNKNOWN, LEAVE UNFORGETTABLE

David was one of the greatest kings of all time. He was also one of the most unlikely kings of all time. When he was young, his dad would send him out into the fields to watch the sheep. Now, this wasn't like asking your kids to feed the dog or take out the trash. This was something a loving parent would never have done. It was dangerous. Shepherds were under real threat of attacks from wild animals and the elements. It was not a highly esteemed position.

So, when a prophet, Samuel, came to see Jesse, David's father, to meet all of his sons to find the potential new king, David was not among them. Simon quickly deduced that the next king was not one of David's brothers. He pressed Jesse about other children, and only reluctantly did Jesse introduce David to Samuel, who knew at once that he had found what he was looking for.

David didn't have anyone else tell him he was great. Even after being anointed and showing up to take down Goliath, King Saul says, "But you're just a kid."

However, David knew better. He didn't need to hear from his father or his king that he had greatness within him. He had put in the work. He had protected sheep from bears and lions and would soon protect an entire race from a giant. He knew what was within him.

Do you? Do you spend your days waiting for others to commend your work? Your efforts? Your appearance? Or do you run into your day without regard for others' commendation? Are you able to find your greatness within?

David's story brings to mind another kid who got off to a pretty rough start. He was diagnosed with attention deficit disorder—ADD—and was put on Ritalin to try to contain his nervous energy. His parents' divorce just wrecked his life. While he was wrestling with all of that, he started to grow. Well, his arms did, anyway. His hands would hang down past his knees and, before long, he became a verbal punching bag for immature kids who decided they had a right to make fun of this kid.

Then, one day, everything changed. A coach approached him and asked if he'd ever tried swimming. "I think you'd be pretty good at it," said the coach.

Coach was right. Michael Phelps, the said long-armed kid, was the youngest swimmer on Team USA at the 2000 Olympics. While he didn't medal that year, the rest of the story speaks for itself. Today, he is the most decorated Olympian of all time.

When he showed up, he was just a gangly kid trying to grow into his body and his sport. Over time, he left an indelible mark on the sport of swimming and in the hearts of fans, inspired kids, and fellow athletes around the world.

No one knew David or Michael when they arrived on their respective scenes. But those two boys knew there was greatness within them, and greatness doesn't know how to quit. They may have arrived unknown, but they left unforgettable.

What do you believe about your greatness—the potential for or lack thereof? The fact is, as a child of the Living God, you have everything you need to be great. You lack nothing. The challenge will be to abandon your excuses, ignore the judgment of the world, and live into your purpose. Take Jesus with you on your journey to greatness, and don't ever look back.

The Big Idea

Greatness isn't born. Greatness is made.
What is holding you back from embracing
all that God has placed within you?
Are you waiting for the affirmation of others?
Is the path you're on leading to a life of greatness or regret?
What will it take for you to leap into the life God desires for you?

Prayer

*Lord, as Your child, I know I have the Author of the universe,
the Perfecter of grace and peace and power, within me. Help
me to trust the potential You have placed inside of me that
I may use it to maximize my life for Your purpose.*

AVAIL +

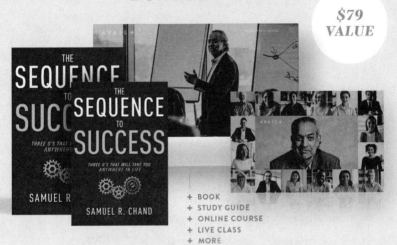

FOLLOW

THE

LEADER

STAY CONNECTED

AVAIL
PODCAST

THE AVAIL LEADERSHIP PODCAST

HOSTED BY VIRGIL SIERRA